Richard Deiss, Nick Snipes

The Gingerbread Station at the other End of the World

**Short stories about 222 railway
stations in Africa, Asia and Oceania**

Address of the authors:

Machnower Str. 65
14165 Berlin
Richard.deiss@gmail.com; nick818ns@yahoo.com

Cover picture:

Melbourne Flinders Station
http://en.wikipedia.org/wiki/File:Flinders_street_train_station_melbourne.jpg
(Autor: Adam J.W.C, Creative Commons Attribution-Share Alike 2.5)

Bahnhof Beijing West (Cover)
http://en.wikipedia.org/wiki/File:Beijing_West_train_station_01.jpg
(Autor: Kim S. Creative Commons Attribute Share Alike 2.0 Gneeric license)

Inside first page: Station of Sylhet, Source:
http://sylhoti.multiply.com/photos/album/16/Beauty_of_sylhet#28

Herstellung und Verlag: Books on Demand GmbH,
Norderstedt
First English language edition 2020, Originalausgabe

Der Inhalt des Buches gibt ausschließlich die Privatmeinung der Autoren wieder. The content of the book represents the private opinion of the authors.

Printed in Germany

ISBN   978-3-746-0611-39

Bibliografische Information der Deutschen Nationalbibliothek
Die Deutsche Nationalbibliothek verzeichnet diese Publikation in der Deutschen Nationalbibliografie; detaillierte bibliografische Daten sind im Internet über http://dnb.d-nb.de abrufbar

Content

Preface

In the summer of 2007, I published the paperback *Palast der tausend Winde and Stachelbeerbahnhof* (*Palace of a Thousand Winds and the Gooseberry Train Station*), which contained little stories, interesting facts, and anecdotes about 200 railway stations worldwide. Over time, more anecdotes were collected, and so, I published my own volume for non-European stations, *Der Lebkuchenbahnhof am Ende der Welt* (*The Gingerbread Station at the End of the World*), at the end of 2008.

In the meantime, more stories have been added, and in summer 2009, I published anecdotes about American railway stations in a third paperback entitled *Grand Central Terminal and the Station at the End of the World*.

This meant that a new edition of the book *The Gingerbread Station at the End of the World* became necessary. In order to fill the gaps left by taking out the American stations, the chapters on stations in Japan, China, India, and Turkey were expanded. The corresponding book was published in autumn 2009, with an update in 2011. This is now a slightly updated new English language edition of the book for 2020. The present book thus contains anecdotes and facts about 222 stations in Africa, Asia, and Oceania. About every two years, the book will be updated. Hints for further interesting stories, anecdotes, and facts about railway stations are always welcome.

The five railway station books together contain stories, anecdotes, and facts about 1001 stations.

Berlin, October 2020
Richard Deiss with Nick Snipes

1. Africa

Africa has never had a well-developed railway network. In colonial times, in many regions, there were only branch lines from the ports to the hinterland to ensure the transport of raw materials. After the end of colonial times, the railway infrastructure in many countries fell into disrepair, partly because it was identified with colonial rule. Today, the railway is of little importance in Africa. The exceptions are Egypt—where more than half of Africa's 80 billion passenger-kilometres of rail passenger traffic per year is taking place—and South Africa (15% of Africa's rail passenger traffic and 80% of its rail freight traffic). Additionally, only the railways of Algeria, Morocco and Tunisia have a transport performance of more than 1 billion passenger-kilometres. In Egypt, the concentration of the population in the Nile Valley favours rail transport. A high number of passengers is reached on a small network. The timetable is dense, and passenger numbers are high. Among the Maghreb countries, Morocco has the densest rail traffic with about four billion passenger-kilometres per year, twice as much as ten years ago. Rail traffic in Tunisia has also increased in the last ten years by about a quarter. In Algeria, after having fallen at the beginning of the millennium, rail traffic is also increasing again. Rail traffic is also growing in many sub-Saharan countries as a result of investment in new rail infrastructure by China (notably in Kenya and Nigeria).

Since sub-Saharan Africa is also rich in raw materials, new railway lines for freight transport are being built or extended there today, above all, with Chinese assistance. Passenger transport has started to benefit from these measures, notably in Kenya and Nigeria, and some stations are also being revitalized or newly built as a result.

1.1 North Africa

Alexandria Misr railway station

Alexandria had the first railway station in Africa, and today's station is also one of the most impressive in the continent. In 1853, Robert Stephenson, son of the famous British railway pioneer George Stephenson, began to build Africa's first railway line from Alexandria to Cairo. The station is called Misr Station "Station of Egypt," after the Egyptian name of the country.

Cairo Ramses Station

In 1958, just a few years after the Suez crisis, Egyptian director Youssef Chahine made the feature film *Cairo Station*, set in Cairo's main railway station. In the film, a handicapped man who works in a newspaper stand named Kenawi falls in love with the beautiful Hanuma. When he tries to win her over with his vision of a traditional quiet country life, she says, "We have got used to the trains and the noise." The film was banned in Egypt for twelve years because of its relatively free-spirited approach to the country's identity and female charms. In today's increasingly "Islamizing" Egypt, it would certainly meet with strong rejection again in some circles because the leading actress appears in shorts in the film.

Cairo's central station had already made women's rights history in 1923 when the Egyptian feminist Hoda Shaarawi (1879-1947) demonstratively removed her veil here on her return to Europe from a Suffragettes congress in Rome.

Today, the station is called Ramses Station. However, a large statue of Ramses II on the station forecourt was moved to a museum in Giza in 2007 due to the effects of exhaust fumes and vibrations.

Oran's neo-Moorish station

The Algerian port city of Oran has one of the most beautiful railway stations in Africa. Designed in the Moorish style, the station resembles a mosque. The square ground plan of the clock tower corresponds to the architectural style of minarets in the Maghreb (which, however, do not have a clock). As in a mosque, a round dome arches over the waiting area. With a design that fits perfectly into the local architectural tradition, it is surprising that the builder was French: the architect Marius Toudoire (1852-1912), who became famous for the Gare de Lyon in Paris. Details of the station show, however, that no Muslim architect could have been present here as the doors and windows are decorated with the Star of David and the ceiling paintings in the entrance hall show Christian crosses.

Toudoire also designed the stations of Bordeaux Saint Jean and Toulouse Matabiou and the post office in Algiers.

The new station of Marrakesh

Marrakesh is in the process of benefiting particularly from the expansion of rail transport in Morocco. In the long term, high-speed rail services to Casablanca and a new railway line to the south are planned. In October 2008, a new Marrakech terminus station was opened. The reception building imitates the architecture of the massive gates of the old town of Marrakesh. The station thus lives up to its role as the gateway to the city. Despite its oriental architecture, the French-speaking railway administration did not miss the opportunity to give the station a new-fangled English name. It is officially called the Marrakesh Rail Center.

Addis Ababa

Addis Ababa has one of the most beautiful railway stations in Africa. However, no trains leave from here anymore, and a road project endangers the preservation of the station function.

In the station square, the gilded sculpture of the Lion of Judah stands on a black granite pedestal. By the way, this lion is also found in the coat of arms of the city of Jerusalem because Judah was an Israeli tribe. The pedestal is decorated with relief portraits of the Ethiopian emperors Menelik II and Haile Selassie I. The statue was erected in 1930, shortly before the coronation of Haile Selassie. Yet, in 1935, the Italian occupying forces took it to Rome. There, the fourth anniversary of the proclamation of the Italian Empire by Mussolini and Adolf Hitler was celebrated. The young Ethiopian Zerai Deres took part in the parade and was supposed to greet the Duce, the Führer, and the Italian King with a ceremonial sword. However, when the parade passed by the lion statue and Deres saw that the national symbol dear to him had been stolen from his country and brought to Italy, he was overcome with rage and stabbed Italian soldiers marching along with his sword. Deres was killed but has since been considered an Ethiopian patriot. In the 1960s, the lion statue was finally returned to the Ethiopians and solemnly reinstated in the station square with the participation of Emperor Haile Selassie. After the 1974 revolution, the new regime under Mengistu wanted the lion removed from the square. However, war veterans reminded Mengistu that an Ethiopian patriot gave his life for the monument, and the lion remained in the station square.

Dire Dawa

Dire Dawa, Ethiopia's second-largest city, owes its existence to the construction of the railway line from Djibouti to Addis Ababa. Originally, the railway line was supposed to run through the city of Harar. For the Muslims of Ethiopia, Harar is the fourth holiest Islamic city after Mecca, Medina, and Jerusalem. Harar was once considered the "Timbuktu of the East" and was not accessible to Christians in the 19th century. Out of consideration for this, Italian and French skilled workers and engineers were settled in nearby Dire Dawa, which was to become a repair and inspection site. As the costs of building the railway exploded, it was decided to run the line along the ridge instead of via Harar. Dire Dawa became the administrative centre of the railway line, which soon attracted the country's foreign trade. The old caravan route from Harar to the coast quickly lost its importance. In front of Dire Dawa station, built in 1902, a grey freight diesel locomotive stands as a monument.

Agordat - from station to airport

The Eritrea Railway, the only railway line in Eritrea, was built by the Italian colonial masters between 1887 and 1932. Many stations on this railway line, including that of the capital Asmara, resemble stations in southern Italy. The railway line from the port of Massawa to Asmara once continued to Agordat and Bishia, not far from the border with Sudan. The station building at Agordat station is still standing but is no longer designed for railway traffic. In the meantime, it is one of a kind and serves as a passenger terminal for the small Agordat airport.

1.3 West- and Central Africa

The monument at Dakar station

Dakar railway station, built in 1914, has several peculiarities by West African standards. On the one hand, there is international rail traffic (to Bamako in Mali); on the other hand, there is regular suburban traffic, both of which are rather rare south of the Sahara. The bronze war memorial in the railway station square - showing a Frenchman and a Senegalese man standing together, with the latter carrying a weapon - is also rather unusual. Next to the soldier Dupont stands the Senegalese marksman Demba. The station square, formerly known as Place de la Gare Dakar-Niger, was renamed Place du Tirailleur in August 2004.

Bamako and the Super Rail Band

In 1970, Tidiane Koné founded the Orchestre du buffet de la gare de Bamako in Bamako, which performed twice a week in the dining hall of Bamako station, the terminus of the Dakar-Niger train line. This was soon to become the most musically influential band in the country. Singers like Mory Kanté and Salif Keit, who joined the band in the early seventies, later became internationally famous. The cover of the band's first records featured the Bamako railway station. Additionally, the Malian Railway Company served as a sponsor for the band. In 1985, the band, which still exists today, took on the shorter and more international name: Super Rail Band.

Bobo Dioulasso and the acronym

Bobo Dioulasso's railway station, built in 1934 in the Sudanese style, is considered one of the most beautiful in Africa. In the last 20 years, its white façade has borne the logos of three different railway companies. In colonial times and until 1989, the international railway line was operated by the Régie des Chemins de Fer Abidjan-Niger. Despite its name, the railway only connected Côte d'Ivoire with Upper Volta. An extension to Niger and the Volta river did not succeed. In 1990, this company was split into two national companies. The Upper Volta was now called Burkina Faso (Land of the Incorruptible), and in 1984, the young revolutionary president Thomas Sankara renamed the railway. The country's railway was accordingly called Société des Chemins der Fer du Burkina (SCFB). A corresponding acronym was displayed at the station. In 1992, the governments of the two countries decided to reunite and privatize the railway. In 1993, a tender was won by SITARAIL, a company based in Abidjan. Today, SITARAIL is part of the French Bolloré Group. The beautiful Bobo station is now adorned with the SITARAIL logo, with a letter on one of the jagged roofs of the station.

Douala-Bessengué - Europe in miniature

Cameroon is also known as "Africa in miniature" because of its scenic, linguistic, and ethnic diversity. However, the country's railway stations would, in some ways, justify the title "Europe in miniature." One example is Douala-Bessengué, the station in the country's largest city. This new railway station houses a fitness centre, has intercity connections to the capital Yaoundé, and—with its modern architecture—could also stand in a major European city. The rail service is operated by Camrail, which belongs to Comazar, a Belgian-South African company. As Cameroon features French and English speakers, the words "Gare" and "Station" are located on the station building. However, in the tribal language of the Bassa and Beti, who live in the south of the country, a third word is used: Banop (station).

Banop originates from the German colonial period (which ended in Cameroon in 1919). The Germans built the first railway lines and stations in Cameroon.

Pointe Noire in Congo

The capital of the former French Congo, Brazzaville (named after the French explorer Pierre Savorgnan de Brazza), is located above the Congo River's current thresholds, which prevents water transport to the seaports. Additionally, the mouth of the river lies in the neighbouring former Belgian Congo. In 1926, the French colonial masters began building a railway from Brazzaville to the port of Pointe Noire. Despite difficulties and the death of many lineworkers from tropical diseases, the project was ruthlessly pushed through. The line was completed in 1934 and is said to have cost 60,000 people their lives. At the time, the French writer André Gide wrote, "the Brazzaville-Ocean railway is a terrible destroyer of human lives." The Pointe Noire reception building does not show the hardship. With its well-proportioned architecture, tiled roofs, and clock tower, it looks like it belongs in a spa town (it is said to be an imitation of the station of the seaside resort of Deauville in Normandy, but it actually does not resemble it in the slightest) and is one of the most beautiful reception buildings in Africa.

Pointe Noire station

Lubumbashi and the lack of hope

Only a few years ago, "Lumumbashi Wantashi" and "Ville d'Esperance" could be read at the train station of Lubumbashi, the capital of the southern Congolese copper province Katanga.

Lubumbashi, which under the Belgian colonial rulers was called Elisabethville, is named after the first prime minister of the Congo Patrice Lumumba, who was assassinated in 1961. Ville d'Esperance (City of Hope) is the nickname of the city. On the other hand, Wantashi is the Kiswahili word for excellence. It is used by several companies in the region as part of the company name. There is also a Wantashi station in Lubumbashi. This station was closed down by the police in early 2010 because it broadcasted a program, which sympathized with separatists (the land rich Katanga province had split from the central government in 1960-1963), a political taboo in the country. Not only the station was closed, but the word Wantashi was also removed from the station's façade, along with the words Ville d'Esperance to remove any hope for independence.

Juba (Southern Sudan)

At the end of the 1980s, the North German railway official Klaus Thormälen quit his job with the railway in order to set up his own welding technology business. Today, Thormälen's company has 400 employees and generates a profit of 100 million euros per year. Yet, he once had even larger plans. In 2003, a plumber arrived at Thormälen's manor house in Trittau, Germany, to fix a broken pipe. The plumber told Thormälen about a German-educated Sudanese man who was visiting nearby and was interested in the railway. Shortly afterward, the Sudanese man visited Thormälen. It turned out that Costello Garang Ring was the son of the king of the most powerful tribe in Southern

Sudan. He told them about the oil deposits in Southern Sudan, which could be used to finance the construction of a railway line. At the time, Southern Sudan, populated by black African Christians and animists, was striving for independence from the Arab-Islamic north. Independence was finally achieved on 9 July 2011. A railway line via Uganda to the Kenyan port of Mombasa would serve as a key element to help develop the new country. Juba is the new capital of the country. Today, there are only huts and a few metres of asphalt roads, but with the railway, the city would also get a station. Thormälen, fascinated by the situation, has since been actively pursuing the Southern Sudanese railway plans. However, the unstable political situation in South Sudan since 2011 and lack of interest in neighboring countries has not yet permitted to progress on these plans. If it will ever be realized it will probably be financed and built by China.

1.4 East Africa

Nairobi and Karen Blixen

Nairobi, Kenya, owes its existence to the railway. In 1896, the British began building the Uganda Railway, which was to connect the port of Mombasa with Uganda: the "Pearl of Africa." Because of difficulties during construction, the railway was soon called Lunatic Railway. For example, in 1898, two lions tore 28 African and Indian construction workers apart at night during the construction of a bridge over the Tsavo River. Nairobi sprung up after a railway station was built halfway between Mombasa and Lake Victoria. Nairobi Central Station is now a modest one-story brick building with three gables.

In 1914, the Danish writer Karen (Tania) Blixen (1885-1962), who later became famous for her book *Out of Africa*, arrived at Nairobi station to travel to her husband Bror von Blixen-Finnecke's coffee farm not far from Nairobi. Today, there is a Blixen Café at the station and a Blixen Museum not far from the station.

Nairobi Kibera

Kibera was long considered the largest slum in Kenya and even Africa. Estimates suggested that as many as one million people lived there. More recent studies, however, assume that only 200,000 people live in the relatively compact Kibera. In any case, Kibera is one of Africa's most famous slums. Here, development aid organisations are taking over, and Kibera is considered a test laboratory for measures to improve the quality of life in slums. There is even slum tourism here. In 2009, The French artist JR created an art project here. Black-and-white photographs of facial features of Kibera residents were enlarged enormously and placed in various locations, including on roofs and slopes. Even the Nairobi-Kisumu railway line which runs through Kibera, was decorated with the photos. Along the railway embankment, the lower half of the face appears, while the upper half of the faces appear on the side of the train. When the train passes, the complete image can be seen. Finally the train stopped at Kibera station, which is of little importance to the inhabitants, as minibuses are the backbone of the traffic.

Dodoma

Not only Nairobi but also Dodoma, Tanzania, owes its function as capital to the railway. After the country's independence, the capital function was to be moved to the hinterland, and Dodoma's current location was chosen because it was not only centrally located but also had a railway station. This station was built by the Germans in 1891, which can still be vaguely recognised today by its architecture.

Dar es Salaam

In the course of the construction of the TAZARA (Tanzania-Zambia-Rail) railway line (1969-1975)—which runs from Dar es Salaam to Kapiri Mposhi, Zambia—a new railway station was built in Dar es Salaam, Tanzania, a little away from the city centre. The station building resembles an airport because cars drive up on the first level. On the street front, the city name "Dar Es Salaam" is written in large letters. This name comes from Arabic and means "house of peace," which is a good name for a station building.

Cecil Rhodes and Bulawayo

While the French once tried to take possession of a west-east corridor from Senegal through the African continent, the British were working on a north-south corridor from Egypt to South Africa at the same time. In Sudan, the two colonial powers clashed, but the British eventually prevailed and even laid out the capital Khartoum according to the layout of the British flag. The British imperialist Cecil Rhodes (1853-1902) eventually pushed for the plan to link his homeland's colonial possessions by a Cape-Cairo railway. Rhodes was mainly active in South Africa and in Rhodesia (today's Zimbabwe), which was later named after him. When the southern Rhodesian town of Bulawayo was connected to the railway in 1897, the banner saying, "Our two roads to progress: Railroads and Cecil Rhodes," was displayed in the station.

The TGV at Antananarivo station

The Madagascar (Madarail) railway company is operated by Comazar. Comazar is in the process of renovating the main railway station (Soarano-Bhf) of the capital Antananarivo, built in 1910 by the Frenchman Fouchard. In the autumn of 2007, the young candidate for mayor, Andry Rajoelina, who was also called TGV because of his speed, wanted to hold an election campaign here. The city council did not allow this to happen because the inauguration of public toilets was planned for the same day. Nevertheless, Rajoelina could not be slowed down, and in March 2009, he became the state's leader. By the way, there are still no toilets at the station.

At the end of 2007, a gang of thieves (including two priests) joined the Soarano station police force and stole the rails, endangering the railway operations.

1.5 Southern Africa

The Grasplatz station and the Diamond

In 1907, August Stauch, a Thuringian railway employee suffering from asthma, moved to Lüderitz, German South West Africa, (now Namibia), to help relieve his condition. In 1905, construction of the Lüderitz railway began. This 1067 mm (cape gauge) railway connected the isolated harbour town with Keetmanshoop, 366 km further inland. Two years later, a connection to the capital Windhoek was built. The railwayman Stauch was stationed at Grasplatz station (despite the sparse vegetation, this was called Grasplatz because grass was handled here for the oxen used as draught animals), 24 km from Lüderitz, where he was given the task of keeping the local section of the line free of sand drifts. His assistant Zacharias Zewala had previously worked in a South African diamond mine. Therefore, Stauch asked him to pay attention to special stones in his work. On 10 April 1908, Zewala brought his superior an interesting find. The mining engineer Nissen in Lüderitz confirmed that it was a diamond. Nissen and Stauch quit their jobs and secured a claim at Kolmanskop. At the time, Kolmanskuppe became the richest town in Africa, and Nissen and Stauch became wealthy. However, during the world economic crisis, Stauch became impoverished. A grandson of his still runs a farm in Namibia.

Diamond mining in Kolmanskop was stopped in 1930, and the place fell into disrepair as a ghost town. The railway station and railway line were blown away by the sand. Yet, trains are once again running on the southern railway line today.

Swakopmund

One of the most beautiful railway stations in Africa is located in Swakopmund, Namibia. Built in 1902, when the country was still a German colony, its tower is reminiscent of the upper tower of the Black Forest town of Gengenbach. However, the reception building is no longer used by the railway, as it now houses a luxury hotel.

The architecture of Windhoek's main railway station, built in 1912, is also reminiscent of the German colonial era, as is its address: it is located on the Bahnhof Street (German for train station).

Johannesburg Park Station

Johannesburg Park Station is considered Africa's busiest railway station with 300,000 users per day. Ten percent of the people working in the city centre arrive here daily by train. However, the railway only provides access to the city's east-west axis, including the densely populated Soweto suburb (South West Township), but not to the residential areas of the white middle class in the north. To prepare for the 2010 World Cup, rail transport in the Johannesburg area was expanded as part of the "Gautrain" project. A connection to Pretoria, which crosses the prosperous white suburbs in the north, was opened in 2011.

In multicultural South Africa, commuter trains are often filled with preachers and their followers. A typical train is one in which a Rastaman rants against eating meat, another in which the Shembe sect advocates a return to traditional Zulu values, and a third in which born-again Christians are under the spell of preachers.

Gandhi and the Pietermaritzburg railway station

Mahatma Gandhi (1869-1948) came to Durban, South Africa, in 1893 to work as a legal adviser for the Indian-born merchant Dada Abdulla. In June of the same year, Gandhi made a train journey to the South African capital Pretoria. He purchased a first-class ticket and sat down in an appropriate compartment. In the town of Pietermaritzburg, a European got on board and complained to the conductor because "culis" and non-whites were apparently not allowed to travel in first class. Gandhi protested and showed his ticket. But the train staff said that if he did not leave the compartment voluntarily, they would have to throw him off the train. And so it happened: Gandhi was pushed off the train, and his luggage was thrown onto the platform. The train continued, and Gandhi retreated to the waiting room. This happened during winter, and Gandhi froze miserably in Pietermaritzburg, 600 metres above sea level. Yet, he did not dare to ask the railway staff about his luggage for fear of being humiliated once again. He thought long and hard about whether he should fight for his rights or whether it would be better to return to India. Yet, he stayed in South Africa for more than 20 years, fighting against racial discrimination, among other things.

In Pietermaritzburg, one of South Africa's most beautiful cities, a bronze statue of Gandhi stands today as a reminder of what happened at the railway station in 1893.

When Gandhi finally returned to India in 1915, he used the train frequently, but always travelled in third class. Once, he lost a shoe while boarding a train. He then threw his other shoe at the lost one. He commented that "The poor man who finds the shoe at least now has one pair to use."

Doornfontein Station

When the new Doornfontein railway station was opened in Johannesburg on 11 June 2009 as part of the infrastructure development for the 2010 World Cup, Deputy Minister of Transport Cronin said that railway stations had been neglected in South Africa until then. He added that many were in hardly better condition than some of the country's prisons. Hopefully, the stations can improve to the level of South African airports, which are wonderful destinations.

Kinross and the lovers

One evening in September 2008, a black couple used the trackbed of the disused Kinross railway station in Mpumalanga province for a night of passion. However, the railway line was only closed for passenger traffic, and goods trains still passed through. This was their downfall. A goods train rolled over them, and they died soon after from their injuries.

Maputo - the Eiffel railway station

The railway station of Maputo, the capital of Mozambique, is worth seeing, as it was designed by Gustave Eiffel. In January 2009, the news magazine *Newsweek* included it in a list of the nine best stations in the world. In the 1990s, it was renovated using UN funds and given a new green coat of paint. However, the station does not see much traffic, as the whole of Mozambique has only a few thousand rail passengers a day. Few trains also depart from the station in the important port city of Beira. Completed by the Portuguese in 1966 and immortalized on the country's 500 Meticais coin in the 1990s, the station building is oversized for just one track and little traffic.

2. Japan

Japan's railways carry almost half of the world's 30 billion annual rail passengers on their small, essentially narrow-gauge network. Tokyo alone, with over 4 billion, has about one-eighth of all rail passengers worldwide. This is due to the dense network of suburban railways in the world's largest conurbation, which complements the inner-city underground network.

Door-closing melodies contribute to a rapid passenger change. They are also necessary, as items of clothing of people who have bid farewell to passengers have already been clamped, and people have been dragged along by the train. The railway companies use different melodies (sometimes even differentiated according to train type). Meanwhile, there are collectors for these tones, and the door closing signals can also be purchased as ring tones. This is not surprising, as Japan is the world's largest music market after the USA, and even ranks first for classical music. Music is also used in traffic. In Japan, there is even a road with grooves that produce a melody when driven over at the right speed. These examples illustrate the Japanese's love of technology, which has also led to a specific railway culture. The Japanese like perfect mechanics, automats, and robots above all. The penchant for automats leads to vending machines with sometimes abstruse offers (like beetles), and long discussions in internet forums whether there really were once such machines for used lingerie. But Japanese people are also romantic and like cute things. This can be seen in a dog monument at a Tokyo station and a cat as an honorary stationmaster.

2.1 Stations in the Tokyo area

Yokohama

Yokohama was the first Japanese city to be opened to foreigners. Many innovations coming from abroad were first used in Yokohama in the 19th century, such as gas lighting. The first Japanese train left Yokohama in May 1872 for Shimbashi Station in Tokyo. All that remains of this first Japanese station is a memorial plaque in front of Sakuragicho Station in Yokohama.

In April 1951, an accident occurred in this station. A train coming in scraped a loosely hanging overhead line. As a result, there was a short circuit, and the train caught fire. 106 passengers were burned, and 92 were injured.

Shimbashi

Shimbashi was the Tokyo terminus of the first Japanese railway line. Since 1872, this line connected the Japanese capital with the port city of Yokohama. In 1914, passenger traffic was transferred to Tokyo station, and Shimbashi became Shiodome freight station. In 1986, the freight station was closed. The site was finally made ready for new construction in 1995. The original platform and several railway memorabilia were discovered. In 2003, a building in the style of the old station but with a different function was constructed on the former site of the station.

Tokyo Station and Amsterdam

Tokyo Station, opened in 1914, imitates the architecture of Amsterdam Central Station. One just has to remove the towers and battlements - partly a consequence of wartime destruction - of the Dutch model to see the resemblance.

The station was also built to celebrate the victory over Russia in the 1905 war.

In 1921, Japanese Prime Minister Hara Takashi (*1856) was stabbed to death in the station by a switchman of a different political orientation. A memorial plaque in the station commemorates the incident.

Shinjuku

Tokyo Shinjuku is considered the world's busiest railway station with over three million passengers per day (although transfer passengers are counted twice). Despite the masses of passengers, traffic generally runs smoothly. However, Shinjuku was also the first Japanese station to use pushers to push passengers into subway and suburban train cars.

Harajuku and the Cosplay youth

The station building at Harajuku Station in Tokyo is a neat little half-timbered building dating from 1906, and its neat appearance is a hint of its first special feature: a special, cordoned-off platform for the imperial train is located along the edge of the tracks, although it is being used less and less frequently. The second special feature can be seen on Sundays when all the toilets in the station are blocked. These are used as changing rooms for young people, especially girls, who dress in the hard-to-define Harajuku style (which oscillates between gothic, punk, and manga) developed in the 1990s and who use a bridge at the station as a catwalk.

Shibuya and the faithful dog Hachiko

Hachiko is one of the most famous dogs in Japan. This Akita dog was born in 1923 in the city of Odate. In 1924 he was brought to the Japanese capital by his owner Hidesamuro Ueno, a professor of agricultural science at the University of Tokyo. At the end of each working day, the dog waited at the nearby Shibuya railway station to pick up his master. But Ueno died in May 1925. Despite this, Hachiko continued to run to the station every evening to greet his master, and did so for 11 years, until his death. Hachiko's loyalty and love for his master touched the Japanese, who finally erected a monument to him at Shibuya station while he was still alive. One year later, in 1935, the dog died. He was stuffed and has since been on display at the Science Museum in Tokyo-Ueno. During the war, the bronze statue was melted down for armament purposes. But soon after the war, a society for the reconstruction of the Hachiko Monument was established and in 1948 a new bronze Hachiko was erected. In 2004 this was replaced by a new casting. A similar statue can be found in Odate railway station, the birthplace of Hachiko. The Hachiko Monument is now a popular meeting place, and one exit from Shibuya Station is named after the bronze Hachiko statue. On April 1, 2007, Japan Times magazine reported that the statue was stolen by metal thieves the night before. Some readers were shocked, but it was just an April Fool's joke.

Ueno - where my language is spoken

The Japanese poet Takuboku Ishikawa (1885-1912) wrote the following short poem about the Ueno railway station in northern Tokyo: "When homesickness comes, I go to the Ueno railway station, where my language is spoken."

His statement is due to Ueno station once being the gate to Tohoku, the northeast of the Japanese main island Honshu, where Ishikawa was born. There they speak a special dialect. People from Tohoku not only arrived in Ueno and left from there but also met there when they were homesick to be closer to home and to themselves. Ward announcements were even sometimes spoken in the Tohoku dialect to help people from the region find their way around. At least that is what Hermann Vinke reported in an article on 15 November1985. Ishikawa, who moved from Morioka, the centre of Tohoku, to Tokyo at the age of 20, could hardly live on his poetry and died of tuberculosis at 27.

The French writer Roland Barthes (1915-1980) later wrote about the Ueno station in his 1970 book *L'Empire des signes* (*The Empire of Signs*) and noticed that travellers on skis would set off from here to the north of Japan.

Ueno and the timetable freaks

Tokyo Ueno station is also a meeting place for Japanese rail freaks, who check the punctuality of the trains there with the pocket timetable Jikokuhyo in one hand and a watch in the other.

Despite tight schedules and short stops at stations, trains in Japan are very punctual. However, there have already been accidents due to excessive speeding because train drivers have tried to make up for delays. Engine drivers have also committed suicide because of delays.

Comagomes and the Azaleas

Komagome Station in Tokyo is known for the colourful view from its platforms in April and May each year. During those months, the azalea bushes along the tracks blossom deep pink. Komagome is also the home of the Someiyoshino cherry tree, which blooms especially beautiful in spring. Therefore, the train departure signal of the station uses the melody of a cherry tree song.

The Mitaka Incident

The relatively inconspicuous railway station in Tokyo's Mitaka district was not opened until 1930.

In 1949, however, the station achieved sad fame. An unmanned train with the governor in place raced into the station and killed six people. The reasons were never fully clarified, but it was assumed that it was an act of sabotage by employees of the railway workers' union. The railway employee Keisuke Takeuchi was then sentenced to death. Eighteen years later, he died in his cell from a brain tumor.

Kamiigusa and the Gundam robot

Japan is one of the leading comic nations in the world. Japanese Manga Comics are now even at the top of the popularity scale among younger readers around the world. Besides comics, the Japanese also have a weakness for robots. That is why robots, for example Gundam, are also among the Manga Comic heroes. The Japanese cartoon company Sunrise produces Gundam anime (animated films) and is based in the Tokyo district of Suginami, not far from Kamiigusa station. Therefore, it comes as no surprise that commuters supported Sunrise's plans to have a statue of Gundam erected at the station. In March 2008, the time had come: a three-meter high bronze statue of Gundam was erected at the station entrance. Many hoped that this would also attract tourists to the city district.

Kansai and the bicycle station

In April 2008, the largest bicycle station in the world was opened at Tokyo's Kansai Station. It is an automatic system with 18 underground cylinders that can hold a total of 9400 bicycles. It takes only 30 seconds to drop off and pick up a bicycle.

Ebisu and the god of luck

The Ebisu station in Tokyo's Shibuya district is named after the Yebisu beer that used to be brewed near the station. This in turn derives its name from Ebisu, the god of luck. A bronze statue of the Ebisu god can, therefore, be seen on the station façade.

Tokyo Hamamatsucho and the little man

On the platform of Tokyo's Hamamatsucho railway station, there is a surprising replica of the Brussels Manneken Pis. Like its counterpart in Brussels, the little man from Tokyo is also relieving himself, into a pool of water on the platform. Just like in Brussels, Manneken is always changing his clothes to the delight of the commuters. The Japanese Hikaru Kobayashi donated the statue in 1952 to mark the 80th anniversary of the Japanese Easter railway. At first, the little boy was made of white porcelain. Since 1968, has he is made of a dark bronze.

Another station in the Tokyo area with a sculpture is Yurakucho. Here, the clay figure of a raccoon stands on the platform amidst plants.

2.2 Stations in the Osaka-Nagoya area

Osaka and the Big Man

The Umeda station in Osaka is the third most frequented railway station in the world, with 2.3 million passengers per day. The station complex is connected to Osaka Station, subways, and shopping levels. Therefore, it is no surprise that the fastest pedestrians in Japan are on the move here at 1.6 metres per second. The giant (10x10 m) "Big Man" TV screen serves as a meeting place. In Osaka, they say, "Biggu Man ni aimashou (Let's meet at the Big Man)."

Kyoto - modern railway station in old town

Kyoto was once the capital of Japan and is known for its historical sights and numerous temples. During the Second World War, the city was deliberately spared by the Americans. However, Kyoto's main railway station, built in 1997, breaks with all historical tradition and the height restrictions that otherwise prevail in the city. Conservative politicians, therefore, regarded it as a stain of shame. Its reception building, whose roof imitates the crown of a bamboo forest, houses a multi-story shopping centre, accessible via a cascade of escalators. The railway has tried to get the most out of the property.

Nagoya, the highest station building

This is also true of Nagoya, where there is an even higher station building, which is actually the tallest in the world. The station complex includes two over 50-story office towers. The headquarters of the Central Japan Railway Company (JR Central) is in one of them. The other tower is used as rental space that brings the railway another source of revenue.

Utsunomiya and the Ekiben

Ekiben are plastic boxes with meals available at Japanese railway stations. These containers are called bento and have compartments for various foods. Ekiben originally consisted of rice balls wrapped in bamboo leaves. When trains were slower, journeys took longer, and other food alternatives were less developed, Ekiben played an important role for travellers. Today some passengers eagerly await new Ekiben creations. The first Ekibibe (in the form of rice balls wrapped in seaweed, the onigiri) were sold as early as 1885 at Utsunomiya station, some 50 km north of Tokyo. The town of Utsunomiya is famous in Japan for its gyoza dumplings.

Nikko and Wright

The city of Nikko is located in the mountains, 140 km north of Tokyo. Nikko is a popular tourist destination with many historical buildings. A Buddhist temple, a Shinto shrine, and a mausoleum located in the city are on the UNESCO World Heritage List. The town's JR railway station, built in 1915 (there is a station on the Tobu Line next to it), is also special, as it was designed by the famous American architect Frank Lloyd Wright (1867-1959). Another Japanese building designed by Wright is the Imperial Hotel in Tokyo, built in 1916. In Nikko railway station, there is a guest room - unchanged in its design to this day - which was once used by the emperor when he visited the town. On the first floor of the station, there is another curiosity: a ballroom with a large chandelier.

Shinchi and the Tsunami

On 11 March 2011, a major earthquake and subsequent devastating tsunami devastated the north-east coast of Honshu, killing more than 20,000 people. The tsunami also destroyed the Shinchi railway station, which is located on the Tokyo-Sendai railway line. A train with four wagons was thrown off the tracks and landed upside down. However, the tsunami warning had worked here, and all passengers had already got off beforehand. Several other stations were also destroyed by the tsunami in March 2011, including Ishinomaki in the Minamihama district.

The Okuma station - located on the same railway line, the Joban Line - got off lightly. Yet, nobody is allowed to get off here anymore. Okuma is so close to the nuclear power plant complex of Fukushima-Daiichi, which was destroyed in March 2011, that the entire population had to be evacuated.

The railway station of the large city of Fukushima was not destroyed. It is located inland, 50 km from the coast, and thus relatively far from the damaged power plants.

Near Hiroshima, there was a station called Tsunami. However, it was closed in 2003.

The cat Tama in the station of Kishi

In April 2006, the Wakayama Railway Company made all stations on the Kishigawa Line (which runs south of the main Japanese island of Honshu) unmanned, including the small Kishi station. Employees of companies located near the stations have been given the task of checking that the stations are in order. The merchant Toshiko Koyama was chosen for the Kishi station. Koyama also took care of stray cats, and he was particularly fond of a cat named Tama, which he regularly fed at the station.

Japanese are cat lovers. For example, the cute comic cat Hello Kitty has developed a cult among Japanese women. So, it is no surprise that in January 2007, the railway employees decided to make Tama the official station attendant. The cat was given a stationmaster's cap and tuna daily. In January 2008, she was even promoted to Super Station Master, and was given two cats as "assistants." Furthermore, an "office" was set up for Tama in a former ticket office. These investments have definitely paid off for the railway company. The Japan-wide publicity achieved by the animal stationmaster has increased passenger numbers by more than 10% and has helped the local economy to generate additional revenue of $10 million.

Settsu and carbon dioxide

The city of Settsu and the Hankyo company announced, in October 2008, that they had started working on a plan to transform the city's railway station into a CO_2-neutral station. The first step is to reduce the station's CO_2 emissions from 65 to 30 tonnes per year. These remaining tonnes will be neutralized through emissions trading. Lower

CO2 emissions will be achieved through, among other things, solar panels, energy-saving lifts that recuperate energy when braking, LED lighting, rainwater recovery, and waterless urinals.

Kanazawa and the water meter

The city of Kanazawa (450,000), located on the west coast of the main island of Honshu, was not bombed during World War II, and therefore, still has a lot of its historical architecture. The Tsuzumi Gate at the modern railway station makes references the city's architecture. The gate got its name because its two pillars are reminiscent of traditional Japanese drums (tsuzumi). An artificial stream flows under the gate, which, after a few metres, flows into a waterfall. At the station, a digital clock shows the time. Surprisingly, their numbers are made of water. Computer-controlled water jets reproduce Arabic numerals. Viewed from a certain distance, the individual mini water jets merge into a readable number.

Obama and the president

On the west coast of Honshu lies the medium-sized city of Obama (32 000 inhabitants). During the US presidential election in autumn 2008, the city's inhabitants, under-standably, favoured with the Democratic candidate of the same name. Since then, Obama became US president, and the tourist shop opposite the train station offers, among other things, T-shirts and a rice cake with the president's likeness. November 4th, the day Obama was elected, was declared a public holiday in the city.

The Seikan Tunnel and its stations

In March 1988, the 53.9 km long Seikan Tunnel was opened, connecting the main Japanese island of Honshu with the northern island of Hokkaido. It is three kilometres longer than the Channel Tunnel (although only 23 km is under the sea) and is the longest railway tunnel in the world. The Seikan tunnel, however, suffers from heavy traffic. There is little rail freight traffic in Japan, and the tunnel is not used by the normal-gauge Shinkansen high-speed trains, but by the narrow-gauge trains common in Japan. Thus, despite the tunnel, a train journey from Tokyo to Sapporo takes more than 10 hours, which is no competition when compared to the plane. There were once two stations in the tunnel - the first submarine stations in the world - which served as emergency stations. They also contained railway museums. One station was already demolished for the installation of the normal-gauge high-speed line through the tunnel, but individual trains still stop daily at the Tappi-Kaitei tunnel station.

Sapporo's old railway station

Japan is also called the land of the eight islands, but Hokkaido is not counted among these islands because it does not belong to the historical core of Japan. The Ainu people were the original inhabitants of the island, and the Japanese did not settle there until the 19th century to prevent it from falling into the hands of the expanding Russian Empire. Sapporo, the largest city of Hokkaido, was connected to the railway in 1880 and was the terminal station at that time. The station burned down in 1907 and was rebuilt in 1908. A replica (on a smaller scale) of this station can be seen in the Historical Village of Hokkaido.

Sapporos new railway station and its tower

In 1951, the half-timbered station built in 1908 was replaced by a modern concrete building. In 2003, this had to make way for a new building with an adjoining office tower (real estate is an important source of income for JR Railway). This 173 m high office block belonging to the railway is the highest building in Hokkaido. On the 38th floor, the urinals in the men's lavatory are arranged in such a way that you can enjoy the view over the city and the railway station while relieving yourself.

Kushiro-Shari and the ice floes

In the north of Hokkaido, the climate is very harsh. In winter, it is characterized by cold air coming from Siberia, and even ice floes float along the coast.

The Norokko train runs twice daily along the north-west coast of Hokkaido between January and March. The station of Kitahama is the closest to the sea. The trains stop here for an extended period so passengers can climb a viewing platform to see the ice floes in the Sea of Okhotsk. The stationmaster's office has been converted into a café, whose walls are covered by greeting cards and tickets left by visitors from all over the world.

Kawayu-Onsen and the foot bath

Kawayu-Onsen in eastern Hokkaido is known for its sulfur springs. The town's railway station has a special feature. The wooden reception building, finished in 1936, houses a foot bath fed by local hot spring water, which passengers can use to relax.

Huis ten Bosch (near Nagasaki)

Tokyo Central Station was modeled on Amsterdam Central Station, but this is hardly recognizable today. The Huis ten Bosch station, a Dutch theme park not far from Nagasaki (40 minutes by train, with its own Huis ten Bosch Express train), has a much more Dutch feel. One hotel in this mini-Holland is even modeled on the Amsterdam Central Station, but with several floors added to maximize the number of beds. It is questionable whether this is still needed today, as the number of visitors has fallen sharply in recent years.

The Hikyo station of Akase

In Japan, there is a special word for remote stations or stops that are hardly served by trains. These are called Hikyo stations. They are particularly attractive to train fans when located in beautiful landscapes, the vegetation is taking over, and fewer passengers board the trains there. The Japanese railway fan Takanobu Ushiyama made the phenomenon of Hikyo stations known in recent years through a corresponding website and his 2001 book. This resulted in a growing number of Hikyo fans and Hikyo visitors. An example of a Hikyo station is Akase station on the Misumi line on Kyushu island.

3. Other countries of East Asia

Asia is the railway continent of the future. China and India are the countries with the highest rail passenger transport performance (India 1200, China 1500 billion passenger-kilometres, more than 60% of world rail passenger transport altogether), followed by Japan. While rail transport in Japan is stagnating, rail passenger transport in India and China is rapidly growing. As the number of cars increases, the roads in these densely populated countries will soon be so congested that only the railways can ensure rapid progress. This is already the case in Japan, where a very dense (narrow-gauge) rail network carries billions of commuters annually, especially in suburban traffic. The development of an intensively used local rail transport system is also becoming apparent in Indian cities such as Mumbai and Kolkata. Today, however, most investment in rail is being made in China. In recent years, huge new stations have been built in Beijing and Shanghai, and a high-speed network is under construction. China is also the first country to have a magnetic levitation train. In addition to Japan and China (since 2008), high-speed lines now also exist in Korea and Taiwan. Some are planned for India. There is still little international rail transport in Asia, but on the Southeast Asian mainland, passenger rail transport is planned from Thailand, via Cambodia and Vietnam, to China.

However, the most beautiful stations in Asia are not the modern stations built for the new lines, but those built in a pseudo-oriental style by European architects during colonial times, such as in Mumbai, Chennai, and Kuala Lumpur.

3.1 North Korea

Pyongyang and Kim Jong Il

A portrait of former President Kim I-sung along the words, "Long live the Great Leader Comrade Kim Il Sung," is displayed on the facade of Pyongyang's main railway station. This is remarkable Kim, born in 1912, died in 1994. Kim Il-sung's son and successor Kim Jong-il (1942-2011) determined that his father, dead or alive, was the "eternal leader" of Korea. Kim Il Sung's portrait is usually hung in every railway station in North Korea but in a smaller version than in the capital railway station.

The President and the inspiration

The cult of personality related to Kim Il-sung is also evident in the following officially circulated anecdote:

On the evening of 6 February 1962, Kim Il-sung was looking at the ticket office of a small railway station in the mountains when he suddenly had an epiphany. A fare table was hung on the wall. As was usual at that time, the characters were arranged vertically. Kim talked to the station master and advised him to write the fares in Arabic numerals and arrange them from left to right, horizontally. Kim left the station and said he would come back the next morning to look at the new fare table. Early in the morning, he inspected the new table and congratulated the railway staff for the changes made. Finally, he ordered that all stations in the country should introduce such timetables.

Kim Il-sung suffered from a fear of flying. He even traveled abroad (limited to Russia and China and Mongolia) by train.

The explosion at Ryongchon station

In April 2004, an explosion occurred in the station of the North Korean city of Ryongchon when wagons loaded with ammonium nitrate came into contact with the overhead line during shunting. A 15-metre deep explosion crater was created, many people died, and hundreds of buildings were destroyed. According to the Red Cross, which was given exceptional access to the site of the accident, 54 people were killed, and South Korean media reported up to 3000 dead. The North Korean dictator Kim Jong-il had travelled through the station by train from China just a few hours earlier. This fueled speculation that it might have been a planned attack on the leader.

The presidential station in Hyesan

Like his father, Kim Jong-il was said to have suffered from a fear of flying. That is why he only travelled long distances by train. However, this limited his radius of action to the neighbouring countries of Russia and China. He even travelled to Moscow on a special train. When an unscheduled train speeds through Siberia, some railway observers wondered whether the North Korean dictator was on board. Kim Jong-il spent his summer holidays in the mountains in the north of the country, not far from the Chinese border. To get there, Kim had his own railway station built near the city of Hyesan. When the first railway station was first built there in 1985, he complained that it could be seen from China and attacked by Chinese planes. The station was converted into an ammunition factory, and finally, a new and more shameful station was built for Kim in a gorge that was difficult to reach by airplanes. Kim Il-sung also once had his own railway station in the area. This was later demolished.

Kaesong terminal station

Kaesong was once a station on the Seoul-Pyongyang railway line. However, due to the division of Korea, the demarcation line running a few kilometres south of Kaesong interrupted the railway connection between the two cities, and Kaesong became the terminus of the line coming from Pyongyang. Therefore, Kaesong became a symbol of the division of the country, and after the turn of the millennium, there were efforts to turn the terminal station into a through station again. After 50 years of interruption, rail traffic between the two countries has now been resumed, but only trains for the transport of goods are running. In autumn 2008, however, traffic was once again interrupted.

Hamhung

The city of Hamhung suffered more than other cities from the North Korean famine catastrophes of the 1990s, as it was less privileged than the capital and, at the same time, too large to be able to supply itself from the surrounding area. There are reports that 10% of the urban population died from starvation. Google Earth aerial photographs showing mass graves on the outskirts of the city seem to confirm this theory. In 1995, out of desperation, soldiers from Hamhung marched in protest towards the capital. Hamhung had been badly destroyed in the Korean War and was later rebuilt in the socialist prefabricated concrete block style, which is also evident in the city's railway station. Due to the poor supply situation, it was considered dangerous for visitors to stay there until a few years ago, as there were repeated robberies.

3.2 South Korea

Dorasan

The South Korean counterpart of Kaesong is Dorasan station. The station is decorated with pictures showing scenes from the country's railway history, but also pointing to the future. A poster shows a railway line with the inscription, "Not the last station from the South, but the first station towards the North." Another picture shows Kim Jong-il and the South Korean Prime Minister shaking hands in the city on 15 June 2000, in front of a map of a united Korea.

Seoul - the station of the capital

The architect of the Seoul railway station, opened in 1925, was Tsukamoto Yasushi from Japan. Yasushi used Tokyo's main station as his model, and the architect is said to have based the design of the station in Tokyo on the central station in Amsterdam. However, the dome of the station is more reminiscent of that of Antwerp station (the dome used the old Lucerne station as its model). During World War II, Seoul's station also was strategically important for the Japanese. Soldiers were to be transported from there to China. Today, this oldest still existing station in Korea is almost disappearing behind new glass-façade station buildings built for high-speed traffic in 2004.

Gwangmyeong

Gwangmyeong is a suburb of Seoul. Gwangmyeong was originally planned as the terminal station for the KTX high-speed trains and was extended accordingly. However, the terminal station of the high-speed line was eventually built in Seoul. Gwangmyeong station is, therefore, oversized for today's train traffic. That is why railway enthusiasts call it Gwangmyeong Airport.

Yongsan and the waterfall

Yongsan became the terminus of the high-speed trains in the Seoul area. This station was transformed into a huge shopping centre after 2004. From street level, one has to climb a wide staircase with many steps to reach the platform level. On one part of this staircase, a waterfall was installed, which is illuminated by a light show at night.

Daegu

At the beginning of 1950, students and youth groups gathered in Daegu station square to protest against the "communist aggressors," who intended to make the peninsula socialist. By the summer of the same year, the station area had become a gigantic refugee camp. Ten years later, in July 1960, thousands of women, dressed in traditional white, gathered in the station square in Daegu for a meeting of the bereaved of the Korean War. The speech ended with the words, "You, sorrowful souls of the unburied dead, we will weep for you for the next thousand years."

Sinnam - the station of poets

In 2007, for the first time in Asia, a station was named after a poet. The Korean writer Gim Yujeong (1908-1937) died young but left behind a collection of more than 30 works. Sinnam Station, located in Chuncheon (100 km east of Seoul and Gim's birthplace), was named after the poet in 2007.

3.3 China

The railway arrived in China relatively late and initially developed slowly. The old cultural nation of China initially felt that the Europeans had imposed this technology on it. In 1876, an English company built a narrow-gauge line from Shanghai to Wuzong, which the Chinese shut down immediately after the first accident and threw the tracks into the sea. After China became communist in 1949, the planned economy could not avoid the expansion of the railway. With the economic boom triggered by the economic liberalization after 1979, the expansion of the railways has accelerated in the last decades. China is now the world leader in terms of passenger-kilometres carried by rail and second in terms of tonne-kilometres (after the USA). In recent years, more than 1000 km of new railway lines have been opened in China every year, and spectacular railway stations have been built in some of the major cities.

Data on rail transport in China

Year	**2000**	**2005**	**2019**
Stations	5785	5561	Ca. 5500
Network (km)	70057 (01)	75438	140000
Passengers (Million)	1019	1156	3660
Passenger-km (Billion)	447	606	1471
Tonne-km (Billion)	1334	2073	3008

Source: Chinese Railway, Chinese Statistical Office

Beijing railway stations

In the city center of Beijing, the streets have always been strictly north-south and east-west oriented. The whole area was once surrounded by a wall. Today, an underground line follows the former wall, and every direction is covered by a railway station. There is a west station, a south station, an east station, and a north station. The Chinese word for north is Bei. Beijing means "northern capital" (Nanjing means southern capital). Beijing has a Xi, a Bei, a Dong, and a Nan station. The Chinese word for station is Zhan.

	North Bei	
West Xi	**Middle** Zhong	**East** Dong
	South Nan	

Peking's old railway station at Tiananmen Square

On the south side of Tiananmen Square, there is a European-looking former station building, which resembles the stations of Hamburg and Wiesbaden. This station, Qian Men, was opened in 1911 and was once the terminus of a railway line built by Englishmen, starting near the coast in Shenyang and leading towards Beijing. Sir Reginald Flemming Johnston, the teacher of the last Chinese Emperor Puyi, arrived here by train in February 1919. West of it, there was another small station at the Beijing Hankou Railway, which was built by Belgians in 1898-1906 but did not exist for long. In Beijing itself, at the turn of the century, traffic was still handled almost exclusively by muscle power. It is said that twenty percent of the male labour force at that time was employed as rickshaw drivers (bicycles were hardly available in Beijing). For the construction of the railway line to the heart of the capital, the English had insensitively breached the city walls of Beijing. The Chinese found this humiliating, and soon after the revolution, the station was closed down, and a new station (now simply called Beijing Station) was built in a more Chinese style further east, outside the former city walls. The old station now houses shops, restaurants, and a theatre.

Beijing Zhan railway station

Ignoring the European contribution to Beijing's railway station history, Beijing Zhan Railway Station, built in record time in the 1950s, is often referred to as the city's first railway station on Chinese websites. In contrast to the European-looking station on Tiananmen Square, Zhan station explicitly links architecture from the 1950s with traditional Chinese styles. The characters on the roof of the station are said to have been written in Mao's handwriting, while the two turrets were an idea of Prime Minister Zhou Enlai.

The North Station

Beijing's North Railway Station, formerly known as Xizhimen Station, is the oldest in the city still in use. At the place of the station, there was once a passageway in the city wall for drinking water coming from the mountains. Today's station building is a simple, modern architectural structure but is lined with spectacular office buildings. The station is connected to Beijing railway station by an underground ring line. In 1909, the station was the starting point of the first railway line built by the Chinese themselves: the Zhangjia-kou Railway. In 1915, a ring line connected the North Railway Station with Qianmen Station. Today, an underground uses parts of the route of this ring line.

Beijing South Railway Station and the trilobite

Beijing's new Southern Railway Station, the largest railway station in Asia in terms of converted volume, was opened on 1 August 2008, shortly before the start of that year's Olympic Games. 60,000 tonnes of steel were used in the construction, and the oval roof of the station is equipped with solar cells to generate electricity. The shape of the station building has already been compared to a UFO or a trilobite. Trains to Shanghai and the port city of Tianjin depart from the Southern Railway Station. For the 150 rail kilometres to the neighbouring city, the trains— based on the technology of the German ICE (Intercity-Express)— reach a top speed of 350 km/h and make the journey in half an hour.

The bronze statue in Zhangjiakou station

A bronze statue of an engineer stands at the modern southern railway station of Zhangjiakou, a megacity 196 km northwest of Beijing. It depicts Zhan Tianyou, the "Father of Chinese Railways" (1861-1919). Even as a child, Zhan was so talented that he was allowed to go to the US for training at the age of 12 and started studying at Yale University at 17. At 20, he graduated and returned to China. In 1905, when the construction of the Beijing Zhangjiakou Railway (later part of the Trans-Siberian Railway) was started, Zhan was appointed chief engineer. The railway was opened in 1909 and was the first that the Chinese had built on their own. Chinese primary school children still read about the Chinese railway pioneer's achievements today.

Qinglongqiao

Work overload contributed to the relatively early death of the Chinese railway pioneer Zhan Tianyou (also known as Yeme Tien Yow) in 1919. Zhan was buried in Qinglongqiao railway station. It is located 88 km west of Beijing at the point where the Trans-Siberian Railway breaks through the Great Wall of China. The Qinglongqiao station is preserved in its original form and is considered to be a "living fossil of the Chinese railway." In 2005, when the station was renovated, a separate waiting room for women was reinstated and marked as such. If you take the train through the station, you can see the bronze statue of Zhan and his tomb in the form of a station portal not far from the tracks.

The 'German' station of Qingdao

The city of Qingdao was the capital of a German "protectorate" on the East China Sea from 1897 to 1914. In 1900-1901, a railway station was built, which resembled a church with its clock tower and small station hall. From here, one could even take a train journey to Berlin at the beginning of the 20th century. The trains took fourteen days to get there, and on the train, passengers could get German beer and schnitzel. The Germans also built a brewery in Qingdao (then known as Tsingtao) in 1903, and this Germania brewery later became the largest beer producer in China (Tsingtao beer brand). Tsingtao is still the market leader in China today, and the beer is exported to 50 countries, including Germany.

Over the decades, the once tranquil Qingdao grew into a city of over a million inhabitants, and the small German-style railway station was soon supplemented by new buildings, resulting in an incoherent architectural structure. In 1990, the German colonialist station building was even demolished, and when the population resisted, the first Chinese citizens' initiative was born.

When the Olympic Games came to China and Qingdao was planned as a venue for competitions, a big chance was taken to offer visitors a representative entrance to the city. With the exception of the historic reception building, all station buildings were flattened in January 2007, including a 73-metre high skyscraper on the station square, the tracks were torn out and lowered, and the station buildings were rebuilt in the historic style in sandstone to match the old reception building.

The dispute in Mukden station

The Russo-Japanese War (1904-05) saw a battle in Manchuria at Mukden (now Shenyang) in 1905, in which 276,000 Russian soldiers faced 270,000 Japanese. The Japanese won the battle, and a dispute arose between the Russian generals Rennenkampf and Samsonov at Mukden railway station because Rennenkampf allegedly did not provide enough support.

It seems that the two did not forget this dispute even nine years later because, at the Battle of Tannenberg in the First World War, the cooperation between the two Russian generals again failed, and therefore, the German troops won the battle.

Shenyang's Sunbird

In 1978, a 7200-year-old wooden sculpture of a bird carrying a sun in its wings was excavated in Shenyang. This sunbird has since become the symbol of Shenyang. A statue of the sunbird also stands in front of the city's railway station.

Shenyang's station copy

The architecture of Tokyo station is said to have been modelled on Amsterdam's main railway station. A hotel building in Holland Park near Nagasaki is even more clearly based on this architectural model. However, the most exact copy of Amsterdam Central Station is in Shenyang, where it was built at a 1:1 scale. However, it does not serve as a station but as a restaurant in the residential area of Holland Village, which was built around the year 2000 by the Dutch-Chinese entrepreneur Yang Bin as a Holland theme park. Since Yang Bin was arrested for fraud in 2003, Holland Village has stagnated and is slowly decaying.

Shaoshan's 'Great Leader

Mao Zedong (Mao Tsetung, 1893-1976) was born as the eldest son of a farming family in the village of Shaoshan in Hunan Province. From 1949, Mao was chairman of the Chinese Communist Party. Because of the growing number of visitors to his hometown, a railway line was opened in 1967 from Changchun to Shaoshan. A portrait of Mao has been hanging on the façade of the railway station in Shaoshan ever since.

The following words were also painted on the wall in the station, "Mao was a great Marxist, a great proletarian revolutionary, a great tactician and theorist." Mao died in September 1976, and a commemorative stamp from that year also shows Shaoshan railway station. Under Mao's successor, Deng Xiaoping, economic liberalization began, and Mao's ideology became less important. The number of visitors to Shaoshan, which in the 1970s was still three million per year, fell sharply, and the train service from Changchun to Shaoshan was greatly reduced.

Wuhan and the sine wave

Wuhan's new station has an impressive, curved roof. On the one hand, this is supposed to be inspired by the wings of the yellow crane, Wuhan's symbolic animal. On the other hand, the roof reflects mathematical equations, as the central dome has the shape of a sine curve. The station, designed by the Paris-based AREP office, was completed in December 2009.

Shanghai South Station

Shanghai South Station, opened in 2006, was considered the only major circular railway station (until Beijing South was opened). A round roof with a diameter of 278 metres, whose steel supporting structure is covered with white plastic weather protection panels, spans the departure hall. Despite the country's technical progress, the special plastic Lexan needed for this had to be imported from Italy, the home of Marco Polo, who once travelled to China.

Nanchang's "Blue Planet"

To celebrate the renovation of the west side of Nanchang station square, a large illusory globe was installed there. As is often the case in Europe, the illumination is in blue to deter drug users (who can hardly find their veins due to the light). But the colour blue also matches the blue planet, whose surface is covered by oceans to more than 70%.

Lhasa railway station and the Tibet line

The fact that 40,000 camels were still being used to transport goods from Beijing to Tibet in 1951 shows just how difficult transport was to the "roof of the world." Every kilometre cost twelve camels their lives. In July 2006, the new railway connection to Tibet was opened. This was a pioneering achievement given the difficult ground conditions as a large part of the shots had to be laid on permafrost, which thaws on the surface in summer. Because of the high altitude above the sea, pressure-tight railway wagons are used, and their air is specially enriched with oxygen. There are also hoses under the seats to supply the passengers with oxygen. Because of the intense sunlight, the windows are additionally equipped with UV filters. Nevertheless, passengers must sign a declaration of health before they can board the train. In autumn 2006, two passengers died: a pensioner who had heart problems and a woman, who gave birth to her child in the bathroom. Lhasa's new Tibetan-style railway station is almost oversized, with its four tracks, for the light traffic as only eight trains depart from it per day, including a direct train to Beijing.

Tanggula- the highest station in the world

Since the construction of the Tibet line, China has had the highest railway station in the world, Tanggula Station, which is 5068 m above sea level. Because of the harsh climate and the low population density of the area, this station is unmanned and is controlled by satellites and a neighbouring station. The architecture of the station refers to the shape and colour of the snow-covered peaks of the region.

Kowloon KCR Station

When a new terminal station for the Kowloon-Canton Railway (KCR) was built on the land that had been heaped up in 1974, the old station building (a red brick building with columns, built in 1910) was to be demolished to make way for a new cultural centre. But a Kowloon citizens' initiative did not want to accept the loss and succeeded in getting the memorial association to submit a petition to the governor of the colony. When that did not help, the memorial association even sent 15,000 signatures to the Queen in 1978, hoping for an intervention by the royal family. But the excavators still arrived, and all that remained of the former railway station was the clock tower.

Hsinchu - the 'German' station in Taiwan

With the opening of the north-south high-speed line, Taiwan has acquired several modern railway stations. As for the old stations, the reception building of the city of Hsinchu in the north of the island stands out. It was built by the Japanese architect Matsuzaki in 1913 and is currently the oldest preserved station building in the country. After the Russo-Japanese War, the Japanese, then-colonial masters of the island, began to dominate East Asia. Only a few decades before that, Japan itself was trying to catch up quickly with the state of science and technology reached in Europe. At that time, Germany was a leader in the natural sciences and technology, which is why many Japanese students studied in the country of poets and thinkers. Among them was Matsuzaki Mancho, who designed the station in a German-style with neo-baroque elements. It is not quite clear which station was the model, but some speculate the old station in Heidelberg. Hsinchu's station is still a sight to see in the city today.

The robot in Taipei Central Station

Taipei Central Station is a rather crude building from 1940, but its interior is interesting. Across from the ticket counters is a metal sculpture of a robot warrior. This was made by the staff of Taipei airport from diesel and electric motor parts and was donated to the station. In the ticket hall, there are also showcases with an art exhibition and a railway shop with railway souvenirs from all over Taiwan. It is not known whether this interior contributes to a good "Feng Shui" for the railway station. In any case, after a series of derailments, train delays, and suicides in the summer of 2005, people were so worried that Zen Master Hun Yuan was consulted. He diagnosed that the main entrance to the station was exposed to a white tiger demon. To prevent the demon from entering, the main door of the entrance was moved six metres back. A glass passageway was created between the portal and this door so that passengers now have to pass through two doors. It is not known whether this helped.

Shengsing

Legend has it that the architecture of Shengsing Station, built in 1907 and the highest of the island's main railway network (402 m, as indicated by a monument at the station), is also supposed to reflect Feng Shui principles. The station, located in the Guangdao mountains, is surrounded by nine mountain peaks, each of which has the shape of a tiger's head. The station was thus sitting in a tiger's nest, and its roof was built in a form that was supposed to ward off evil spirits. Unfortunately, the evil spirits of the station could not stop its closure, as the last passenger train stopped here on 23 September 1998.

Kaohisung's mobile station

When a train arrives, you sometimes have the illusion that the station is moving. The Japanese Imperial Crown Style station reception building in the southern Taiwanese port city of Kaohsiung, built in 1941, was actually mobile in 2002. In order to develop the station into a link between high speed, normal long-distance, and local traffic, it was moved by 82.6 m at a speed of 60 cm/hour over a period of fourteen days. The station building, thus, became the temporary entrance to the Gallery of Vision Museum. When the reconstruction work was completed in 2016, the building moved back and become the portal of the new station complex.

Incidentally, Kaohsiung's oldest railway station was the Kaohsiung Harbour Station, now called Kaohsiung Harbour Station. When the new two-story main station was built in 1941, it was still visible from afar in the flat city. In the meantime, however, Kaohsiung has become a city of over a million inhabitants with numerous high-rise buildings.

Fenchihu

Around 1912, the Japanese colonial government built a narrow-gauge forest railway from Chiayi in the coastal plain up to the Alishan mountain region to transport logs. This 762 mm narrow-gauge railway is an adhesion railway, which means that it does not need any cogwheels or standing ropes. Over a distance of 86 km, a difference in altitude of over 2000 m is overcome. When direct road connections were built in the 1980s and the railway became less important, Fenchihu, which is located next to the railway but is difficult to reach by road, experienced a period of decline. Today, it is being rediscovered by tourists and railway enthusiasts due to its railway station and antiquated ticket office, which has been preserved in its original state. The starting point of the journey is often the lowland village of Chayi, where the narrow-gauge tracks of the mountain railway begin.

Guanshan

Taiwan was once a Japanese colony, and the island's first railway lines and stations were built by the Japanese. However, earthquakes and the laying of railway lines mean that little is left of the Japanese architectural heritage. Guanshan has the last station on the east coast line, which is preserved in the northern Japanese village style. However, Trains no longer stop at this station, but instead at a new, relatively coarse concrete structure.

Due to a bicycle circuit around the village, Guanshan has become a popular city for bicycle tourists in recent years.

Toucheng's station square

Toucheng station square is over-furnished in terms of architectural art and monuments. A map of the region showing the seven stations of Toucheng is embedded in the pavement in front of the station. In the small park in front of the station, next to a fishpond, there is a monument commemorating the turn of the millennium. A sculpture crowned by a star was also made from rails at the station, from which water flows. Additionally, a large memorial stone commemorates the first plantation and the first settlement that was established in the area. Despite the many works of art, the reception building itself is a relatively simple concrete building.

3.5 Mongolia

Ulan Bator - the red hero

Mongolia was the second country in the world to become communist after Russia, and without Russia, Mongolia would still be part of China today. The capital of the country is still called "Red Hero (Ulan Bator)," and the characters in the city's railway station, through which the Trans-Mongolian railway (in Russian broad gauge, i.e., 1520 mm) runs, are written Cyrillic and also Latin. Rail travel arrived late into the country; the construction of the Trans-Mongolian Railway, as a connecting line of the Transsib with China, began only in 1947, and the capital Ulan Bator got its first rail connection (in broad gauge) in 1950.

Choir and the cosmonaut

The small Mongolian town of Choir on the Trans-Mongolian railway has a small but not very busy railway station. The station name is written in Cyrillic characters, as is customary in Mongolia. In the station square, there is a statue of the first Mongolian cosmonaut, Jügderdemidiin Gürragchaa, who flew into space from Baikonur in 1981 with a Soviet cosmonaut. Although Gürragchaa did not come from the village, a monument had been erected to him in Choir because there was a Russian airbase there.

Zamyn Üüd

Every year, almost one million people pass through Zamyn Üüd, the beautiful Mongolian border station to China. It was built in 1995 with Japanese help. However, its tower architecture is more reminiscent of Disneyland than traditional Mongolian architecture.

4. South-East Asia

4.1 Thailand

Bangkok Hua Lampong

The main railway station of the Thai capital, Hua Lampong, was built from 1910 to 1916. The reception building was designed by the Italians Tamagno and Rigotti in the Italian neo-Renaissance style. The Germans also had a great influence on the development of the railway system in Thailand at that time; for example, the locomotives were made in Germany. Some people think that they can also see German architectural influences in the reception building. Hua Lampong somewhat resembles the former Berlin Anhalter Bahnhof, however, without the ground floor. Yet, the model was the former Central Station of Manchester, which is an exhibition hall today.

Thonburi Station

The Thonburi railway station in Bangkok, also known as Bangkok Noi and located on the west bank of the Chao Phraya River, could only be reached by water from the city centre for a long time. However, in May 2009, an elevated railway line was opened to this part of the city. The first station building, built in 1900 by the German architect Karl Siegfried Döring, was destroyed by an Allied bombing raid during the Second World War since it was being used by the Japanese as a military base. After the war, it was rebuilt in the original style. In the 2004 film version of *Around the World In 80 Days* starring Jackie Chan, Thonburi Station was used as the railway station of Agra. In 2003, however, the station was moved 800 metres, and the old station building was closed down and sold to the adjacent growing Sirirate Hospital. Bangkok is an expanding media centre with hospitals serving an increasing number of wealthy foreign guests.

The "German" station of Phitsanulok

Phitsanulok in northern Thailand surprisingly has a railway station, which resembles a German half-timbered house. Therefore, it comes as no surprise that the station was built in 1912 by the Cologne architect Karl Siegfried Döring (1879-1941), who also designed the Thonburi Station in Bangkok. However, the former half-timbered architecture has only been preserved in a simplified form.

Hua Hin and the Top 9

In January 2009, the American news magazine *Newsweek* presented a list of the nine best stations worldwide. Only one station in East and South East Asia was on the list: the small station of Hua Hin in Thailand. Hua Hin, located 185 km south of Bangkok, is the oldest seaside resort in Thailand. The upswing began in 1921 with the construction of the railway line from Bangkok to Singapore. In 1926, the royal family established a summer residence in Hua Hin.

In order to provide the royal families with an entrance befitting their status, a pavilion of Sanam Chan Palace was transported from Nakhon Pathon to the railway station and, in 1968, was set up as the royal pavilion. It still stands there today, but kings no longer arrive here.

River Kwai Bridge Station

The Bridge on the River Kwai was a 1957 feature film based on the novel of the same name by Pierre Boulle. In the film, British prisoners of a Japanese POW camp are forced to build a railway bridge over the Kwai River.During the

Second World War, the Japanese actually tried to connect Thailand, which they occupied, with the newly conquered Burma via a railway line. Asian and Allied prisoners of war were used for the construction, and since many died while building the railway from working conditions or tropical disease, it became known as the Death Railway. There is a large military cemetery in Kanchanaburi on the Kwai River, which commemorates the dead. The River Kwai Bridge Station provides direct access to the famous bridge.

Pattaya

The seaside resort of Pattaya, located about 100 km south of Bangkok, is also known as Germany's 18th federal state due to the thousands of German retirees who spend the winter or even the whole year here (Mallorca is already considered the 17th federal state). In March 2009, journalist Alexander Osang from the German magazine *Spiegel* reported on the life of German pensioners in Pattaya. In the article, one man tells the story of how he met his much younger girlfriend at Pattaya station and fell in love with her. Pattaya has a small train station, from which a train to Bangkok departs only once a day. The single-track line with twenty goods trains per day does not allow for dense passenger traffic, but in light of the high number of tourists in the area, it should have more potential than the 50-60 passengers who travel to Bangkok on the single train per day. Bangkok's airport is now connected to the rail network, and if tourists could travel from there to Pattaya with at most one change of train, more vacationers would certainly take advantage of such an offer. However, due to the current thin timetable and the long journey time of four hours, tourists have no choice but to travel to Pattaya by bus or taxi.

Rangoon Fairy Train Station

The main railway station of Rangoon, built by the British in 1877 in the Victorian style, seemed so idyllic, with its majestic lawns, to the inhabitants of the city that they called it "Fairy Station." However, during the Second World War, the station was destroyed by Japanese bombs, and the British retreated to India. The new station, opened in 1954, was built in a traditional Burmese architectural style. It has four towers and is now a historically protected building.

Mandalay Central Station

Mandalay is a centre of Burmese culture and the country's most important railway junction. During the Second World War, even Mandalay's importance as a railway junction grew as the south of the country was occupied by the Japanese. Today, the main railway line from Rangoon ends in Mandalay, and regional lines branch off from here. The city has a modern railway station with an eight-story station building. The number of floors does not seem to be a coincidence because, in the 1980s, many people from southern Chinese came to do business here, and for them, eight is a lucky number.

Pyinmana

In November 2005, Burma's capital function was trans-ferred from Rangoon to Pyinmana, more precisely to an area three kilometres from Pyinmana, now called Naypyidaw. Therefore, the new capital got a railway station. This station was in the spotlight in May 2009 because a bomb is said to have exploded there.

Da Lat's French railway station

In 1912, the French colonial masters of Vietnam founded the pleasantly temperate spa town of Da Lat at an altitude of 1500 metres. The town is characterized by French colonial architecture and even has a small Eiffel Tower. Therefore, Da Lat became known as Little Paris. The station's reception building, opened in 1932, is said to be a copy of the station of the French seaside resort of Deauville. At one time, three trains equipped with cogwheels connected the station with the lowlands every day, and passengers could travel from Saigon continuously on rails. However, the railway line was destroyed by the Vietcong during the Second Indochina War. Since the end of the 1990s, however, the cogwheel connection between Dalat and the village of Tari Mat, eight kilometres away, has been in operation again.

Ho Chi Minh City and Saigon Station

Saigon, the capital of the Republic of Vietnam until 1975, was officially renamed Ho Chi Minh City after the revolutionary and politician (1890-1969) after the union with North Vietnam. But abroad, and also in Vietnam, the city is often still called Saigon. And the letters Ga Saigon (Ga is the Vietnamese word for railway station, derived from the French gare) are also found on the façade of the city's railway station.

Hué

The city of Hué, located in the centre of Vietnam, was the country's capital from 1802 to 1945. The colonial masters had a railway station built here, which seems like a Parisian suburb station. With its red-painted façade, it is now one of the most beautiful stations in the country.

Phnom Penh

The main station of Phnom Penh, Cambodia, built in 1932 by the French colonial masters in Art Deco style, makes a peaceful impression with its cream-yellow facade. Nevertheless, it is linked to the traumatic recent history of the country. In 1960, a secret congress of the revolutionary people's party KPRP with Pol Pot took place on the station grounds. In 1975, Pol Pot's Khmer Rouge took Phnom Penh and began a four-year reign of terror that cost the lives of over a million Cambodians. In 1979, the Khmer Rouge were driven out by the Vietnamese. They fled the city by train from the train station, but Pol Pot himself took a helicopter.

Battambangs Bamboo Trains

Phnom Penn Station sees little rail traffic today. One train a week heads to Battambang, 290 km away. Its station has an Art Deco design. In the Battambang area, there are so-called bamboo trains. These are light rail vehicles, used for informal passenger and freight transport and built by the population themselves, consisting of a bamboo platform, an engine, and two axles.

Tha Nalaeng (Laos)

For a long time, Laos was one of the few countries without a railway and, therefore, without a station. However, on the Thai-Lao Friendship Bridge over the Mekong, the border river between Thailand and Laos, a metre-gauge line was installed in 1994. In March 2009, this was extended to Tha Nalaeng in Laos, which can thus be considered the first railway station in the country.

Kuala Lumpur's oriental fairytale railway station

The old main station of Kuala Lumpur, opened in 1910, has an oriental style, with a white façade and Indo-Saracenesque towers. Its architect was a Briton, Arthur Benison Hubback. Today, however, only local trains stop at the old station, while long-distance traffic is handled at the new Kuala Lumpur Central station.

The Taj Mahal of Ipoh

Ipoh, located 200 km north of Kuala Lumpur and was once rich due to tin mining, also has a magnificent railway station. This station, built in 1915, is even nicknamed the "Taj Mahal of Ipoh." The station is also home to the Ipoh tree, whose poisonous fruit juice was once used to make poisonous arrows.

Singapore - Tanjong Pagar

Tanjong Pagar was Singapore's inner city mainline station for a long time. Yet, until 2004, a "Welcome to Malaysia" sign hung over the entrance. The land on which it stood and the railway corridor to Malaysia was once leased by the Malaysian railway company KTM for 999 years. The city government tried for a long time to persuade KTM to move the station to the outskirts of the city so that the line could fall to Singapore. Therefore, Singapore had already been carrying out passport controls on the outskirts of the city for a few years. Since Malaysia did not participate at first, there were complicated border crossing procedures at times. Since 1 July 2011, however, this has been layered, as the inner city station was closed down, and the Woodlands Train Checkpoint, which has existed since 1903, was converted into a border station.

4.6 Indonesia

Batavia Noord

Indonesia's first train ran from Batavia Noord to Buitenzorg in western Java as early as 1871. Batavia, which corresponds to the Latin version of the country name Holland, was the name of the country's present capital in Dutch colonial times. When Kota Station was opened in 1929, the small Batavia Noord station, of which no traces remain today, was closed down.

Jakarta Kota Station

Today's Kota station in the Indonesian capital Djakarta was called Batavia Benedenstad in Dutch colonial times. Benedenstad is the Dutch word for lower town. When the Dutch colonial masters built railway stations in Indonesia, they sacrificed buffaloes, following local traditions, to give the stations a good future. The Dutch even buried the heads of two water buffaloes near Batavia Central Station in the capital city of Jakarta after its reopening in 1929. When the station was opened, the newspaper Javabote said it was an impressive building and was considered one of the most beautiful stations in the East.

Jakarta Tanjung Priok

The Tanjung Priok port station, built in 1921 and temporarily closed to passenger traffic, was once the most elegant in Indonesia due to its mixture of Art Deco architecture and Indian Classicism and its large platform canopy, the largest in Indonesia. It was here that important figures of the Dutch colonial administration, who had arrived in Indonesia by ship, boarded the train. The station had an underground VIP waiting room, which is no longer accessible today. The station has been seeing passenger trains again for a few years now, and three of the former eight lines now serve it again. A restoration of the building is underway.

Bandung

In Indonesia, before the advent of air conditioning, passenger trains carried ice blocks in crates for refrigeration, which were exchanged at stops in stations. Because of the pleasant climate of the 768-metre-high city of Bandung, the Dutch colonial masters once planned to move Indonesia's capital function here. Government buildings were erected, and streets were built in the Art Deco style. The city was given the nickname "Paris of Java." The city's railway station is unspectacular but is considered the tidiest and cleanest in Indonesia. Numerous locomotives are parked here because the gradient from the lowlands is considerable. Indonesian Railways, railway initiatives, and model railway clubs have their headquarters in Bandung.

Surabaya

Next to Jakarta and Bandung, Surabaya can be considered the most important railway city in Indonesia. Surabaya once had four railway stations. The most historically valuable is the Semut station, whose colonial architecture has been preserved but is no longer used for passenger transport. However, local websites complain about its decay (even the door handles have been unscrewed) and demand that a museum be set up in it. Today, the main station of the city is the Gubeng station, which has been modernized in recent years, and from which, more than 20 passenger trains depart daily.

4.7 The Philippines

Manila Tutuban

In 1886, the Manila Railway Company commissioned Fleming to build a railway line. Several houses had to be demolished for the railway line, which ended at the Tutuban Central Station. Among them was the parental home of Andres Bonifacio (1863-1897), who later got a job at Fleming. Bonifacio later rebelled against the Spanish colonial rule, was executed, and is today considered the "father of the Philippine Revolution." He is honoured in the country as a national hero. In the 1990s, the station building was converted into a shopping centre (but trains still leave the station), and a monument to Bonifacio was erected in the forecourt.

Blumentritt light rail station in Manila

In Manila, there is a light rail transit station of the Manila Light Rail Transit System (MLRT) with the strange German name Blumentritt. It is located on Blumentritt Street, which is named after the Sudeten German teacher Ferdinand Blumentritt (1853-1913). Blumentritt was one of the leading Philippine connoisseurs of his time, although he never visited the island archipelago. Because he was a friend of the Philippine national hero José Rizal (whose day of death, December 30th, is still a holiday), Blumentritt is also well known in the Philippines. Therefore, a street and tram station was named after him. On 30 December 2000 (Rizal Day), the Manila Metro Rail Transit (MRT) area was bombed, and twenty-two people died.

5. South Asia

Rail transport in India

After Japan, India is the country with the most rail passengers worldwide. In 2007, Indian Railways carried over six billion passengers, more than all the railways in Europe combined. In the Bombay area alone, suburban transport carries over one billion passengers each year. In India, the capacity utilization rates of Japanese suburban trains are even partly exceeded. This is also made possible by more spacious railway carriages because India has a broad gauge (1676 mm), while the dense Japanese suburban traffic has to be handled on a narrow-gauge network. India is already ahead of Japan in the number of passenger kilometres travelled. With almost 700 billion passenger kilometres, India accounts for a quarter of the world's rail passenger transport. Because of the greater distances travelled, China, which for a long time was in a neck-and-neck race with India, is now ahead of India with 800 billion passenger kilometres. While India, where a first railway line was opened in Bombay in 1853, had an earlier start than China (first railway in 1876) and was long in the lead in terms of the length of the railway network, China has overtaken India in the last two decades with ambitious expansion programs. China's rail freight performance is six times greater than India's. India does not (yet) have high-speed lines and spectacular new railway stations like those in China. On the other hand, among India's 8000 railway stations, there are many with historically interesting architecture. Additionally, the Indian railway is also making progress. For a long time, it was a loss-maker, but today it makes several billion euros a year in profits.

India

Miscellaneous Facts on Nine Indian Railway Stations

The Indian station with the shortest station name is Ib in Orissa. Venkatanarasinharajuvariapeta, an unmanned station in the state of Andhra Pradesh on the border with Tamil Nadu, has the longest name.

The station with the most long-distance trains is Lucknow, the capital of Uttar Pradesh, where sixty-four long-distance trains depart daily.

Siliguri station is likely to set a new record because it has three gauges: Indian wide gauge (1676 mm), metre gauge, and 610 mm narrow gauge.)

Two stations are located in two states at the same time; the eastern part of Navapur station is in Maharashtra, while the western one in Gujarat. The eastern part of the Bhawani station is again in Madhya Pradesh, while the western part in Rajasthan.

The two Indian railway stations which are closest together are Safilgada and Dayanand Nagar: the distance between the two stations is only 170 metres.

The New Delhi station, which was converted into a modern transport hub by the time of the Commonwealth Games in 2010, has the most extensive switch relay system in the world in its track area.

Mumbai CST (formerly Victoria Station)

The grandiose Mumbai (Bombay) terminus station was opened in 1888 by the British architect Frederick William Stevens. Some people think they see echoes of the architecture of St. Pancras Station in London. There is even a rumour that the building plans were originally intended for Flinders Street Station (Melbourne). In 2004, the station was inscribed on the UNESCO World Heritage List. The architecture is a mixture of Venetian neo-gothic and oriental elements. The heavy monsoon rains run off through the mouths of figures integrated into the facades. It is considered the railway station with the highest number of passengers per day (3 million) outside of Japan. However, a lot of travellers hang from the doors of the overcrowded trains (inside there are up to 15 passengers per square metre) or sit on the roofs, which is not without danger since about 3000 people die every year in Mumbai's suburban traffic.

Bombay/Mumbai CST (Picture: Wikipedia)

Mumbai and the renaming

Originally named after Queen Victoria of Great Britain, Mumbai's neo-Gothic terminus was renamed Chhatrapati Shivaji Terminus (CST) in 1996. Additionally, the city's airport and a museum are also named after it. What is the significance of this name? Shivaji Bhonsale (1630-1680) founded the Maratha Empire in the West Indies in 1664. In 1674, Shivaji was crowned Chhatrapati (king). This Hindu ruler is considered a hero, especially in the state of Maharashtra, where Mumbai is located. Thus it came about that the ruling party in Mumbai, the Hindu *Shiv Sena*, has been busy for several years naming buildings in the city after this ruler, including the venerable Victoria Station, which is still known by its old name.

Mumbbai Churchgate and the Dabbawallahs

Mumbai's second terminus is Churchgate Station, located in the west of the peninsula. It plays an important role in the Dabbawallah system, which provides commuters with hot meals. Dabba means can, which refers to the aluminium or tin cans in which meals are transported. These meals are prepared by the wives of the commuters. The "dabbawallahs" collect these meals from the women in the suburbs before lunch—often by bicycle—take them by train to Mumbai, and hand them over to local dabbawallahs, who hand them over to their wives at the workplace. Every day, 200,000 meals are handed out, and 5000 dabbawallahs, often illiterate, are employed.

Simple colour codes are used to differentiate between the cans. Since so few are misdirected (one in every eight million), logisticians have studied the system, and management researchers have described it as a model of precision. The system is also made possible by the high population density of the city (more than 20,000 inhabitants per km^2), which makes a system based on motorized private transport impossible. Mumbai's dense suburban rail network is another important factor, and despite the full trains, the dabbawallahs still find room to transport the meals.

Hyderabad-Kacheguda - India's most beautiful station?

One of the most beautiful railway stations in South Asia is the Kacheguda Station in Hyderabad. It is one of the three mainline stations in the city and was built at the beginning of the 20th century. With its white oriental style and turrets, it somewhat resembles the station of Kuala Lumpur.

Rameswaram and the cows

Rameswaram is also called Benares of the South and is one of the most important Hindu pilgrimage sites. It is located on an island off the southern tip of India, which is connected to the mainland by a bridge. Rameswaram is a terminus station from where ferries to Sri Lanka depart. Hindus even believe that there was once a land connection to Sri Lanka created by a Hindu god, the Adam's Bridge, which can still be seen in today's island band.

The importance of Rameswaram as a place of pilgrimage is also evident at the railway station. Four stone (holy) cows sit on the façade and roof of the reception building.

Chennai Central Station and the red colour

Chennai Central Station (formerly known as Madras) is considered an important symbolic landmark for Southern Indians. The transport function of the station helped the city to be nicknamed "Gateway to the South." In films from South India, sequences filmed in the station were used for arrival in the city. Most trains from the south arrive at the city's second station, Egmore Station. Despite the Indian architectural style, the station had a British architect in Henry Erwin. The red colour of its façade is supposed to refer to the building material brick. Yet, in 2005, it was painted yellow. However, the citizens of the city could not get used to the change in colour and finally decided to repaint the station in its original red colour.

Chennai Station (Picture: Wikipedia)

5.2 Northern India

Howrah Station and the bridge

The French writer Henri Michaux (1899-1984) once said, "Compared to all the railway stations in the world, Kolkata's railway station is fantastic. It crushes them all. It alone is a railway station." Nearly one million travellers use this huge station every day. However, this is not even the largest railway station in the Kolkata area. An even mightier station, with massive red towers, is in Howrah on the Hoogli River. It receives nearly 1.1 million passengers daily. An endless stream of passengers rolls from this station over the Howrah Bridge into the centre of Kolkata. With two million passers-by and 150,000 vehicles per day, this is considered the busiest bridge in the world. To accommodate the masses of travellers, goods trains are no longer allowed to enter the station, and soon, only travellers will not be allowed to enter. Trains are also getting longer and longer, today up to 25 wagons per train.

Howrah Station (Picture: Wikipedia)

Günter Grass and the taxi driver

The German writer Günter Grass (1927-2015) stayed in Kolkata from August 1986 to January 1987 at the invitation of the local Goethe Institute. Grass saw the problems of the city and called it "God's turd." Grass and his wife Ute initially lived in the suburb of Baruipur, 32 km south of Kolkata. From there, they regularly took the train to Sealdh station in Kolkata. Once, when arriving there, Grass was asked in English by a taxi driver, "Aren't you a writer?" Grass answered, "Yes." Then the taxi driver said, "Didn't you write *The Tin Drum.*" Grass replied, "Yes." Then the taxi driver said, "Then you are Graham Greene."

Kharagpur and the long platform

Kharagpur, a suburb of Kolkata, is known for being the location of the first Indian Institute for Technology. Kharagpur has is also known for another achievement: with a length of 1072 metres, it has the longest railway platform in the world. The trains in India have become longer and longer in recent years.

Lucknow and the wrong monkey

The station in the north Indian city of Lucknow is one of the Indian stations with the highest frequency of long-distance trains. In recent years, however, it has also been heavily frequented by monkeys. When the monkeys even bothered train passengers, the station management looked for a way to get rid of the plague without physically hurting the monkeys (because Hindus worship the monkey god Hanuman). This was achieved in an unusual way. The railway company hired a man in autumn 2008, Achan Miyan, who walked around the station half-naked with his monkey tail on like a primate. He was paid around five euros a day for this. This money was well invested because, during October 2008, this strange monkey man chased the monkeys, who were afraid of him, out of the station.

Varanasi (Benares) and the cycle

On the roof of the station of Varanasi (Benares), one can see a wheel with 24 spokes. It is not an impeller wheel because railway wagons do not have thin spokes. Rather, it is a Hindu-Buddhist symbol that can also be seen on the Indian flag. There are wheel variants with different numbers of spokes and different symbolic meanings, but the 24 spokes are suitable for a station with a 24-hour timetable.

Khusrupur and the riots

The fact that the railway is an important means of transport in India is also shown by the protest of the population when train stops are cancelled. In Bihar, India's socially troubled poorhouse, even a train station was torched. When Indian Railways decided to have fewer trains stop at Khusrupur station from May 2009, protesters set fire to the station and several trains.

Ongole and the Ambedkar bust

In September 2008, a gold-coloured bust of Dr. B.R. Ambedkar (1891-1956) was placed on the platform of Ongole railway station (Andrah Pradesh state). Ambedkar had been particularly committed to the cause of the Dalits, the descendants of the Indian natives, who are considered untouchables in the caste system. Ambedkar, himself born into an untouchable caste and later converted to Buddhism, has been worshipped by the Dalits ever since. At Ambedkar's instigation, the Buddhist wheel was once incorporated into the flag of India.

Bhavnagar

Bhavnagar station in Gujarat is the only one in India where women work as porters. When the city of Bhavnagar got a railway connection in 1880, the ruler of the Bhavnagar region, Taktsinhij Thakor, gave the women of the Koli community the right to work as coolies in the station. Forty women were given badges, which marked them as royal coolies. These badges were passed down from generation to generation to the daughters, who were thus given the opportunity to earn a living. Although the badges are no longer tied to one sex, they are still passed on to daughters only. Even today, 22 women work as porters in the station. A female porter earns about 100 rupees a day (1.50 in euros).

Munabao and the border

Munabao is the last station in the West Indian state of Rajasthan before the border with Pakistan. After the war with the neighbouring country in 1965, the railway connection to Pakistan was interrupted, and the station closed. In 2005, however, the railway station was rebuilt in the course of improved relations between the two countries. As a precautionary measure, it was surrounded by a 3-metre high barbed wire fence, so that no passenger could escape unnoticed. Therefore, the neighbours are not yet completely confident, and Indian security forces patrol the 12 km stretch to the border on foot and with camels.

5.3 India's narrow-gauge mountain railways

Shimla and the toy train

The British colonial officials suffered greatly from the scorching summer heat of northern India (the capital was Calcutta until 1911). They found relief in the coolness of the mountains. From 1834 to 1939, the colonial government of British India moved to Shimla—situated at an altitude of over 2000 metres, on the edge of the Himalayas—during the summer months. Shimla is still characterized by British colonial architecture today. The railway station was Kalka, from where an eight-hour caravan departed. In 1903, a narrow-gauge railway was finally opened between Kalka and Shimla. Due to its narrow 762 mm gauge, it is also called "Toy Train" in India. In 2008, the railway was included in the UNESCO World Heritage List.

Solan Brewery Station

The heat of India made the British thirsty. Since the country provided a market for beer, the Britain Edward Dyer moved to India to open the first brewery in the city of Kasauli. The first beer of the brewery and, thus, of India was called Lion. It was popular with the British, and an advertising poster said it was "as good as back home." Because there was plenty of spring water there, the brewery was soon moved to Solan. Later, the brewery was bought by the British entrepreneur H. G. Meakin, and the company became Meakin and Dyer Breweries. The brewery, located on the Kalka-Shimla railway line, even got its own railway station. When the road to Solan was extended, the transport of goods by rail lost its economic viability because it was necessary to change lanes in the village of Kalka. Therefore, the brewery soon ceased shipping operations. Finally, it was decided that passenger transport would also be discontinued. Yet, passengers can still smell the brewery when the train passes by.

Barog and the tunnel

The longest tunnel of the Shimla-Kalka line is located at Barog station. It is named after the British engineer Barog, who had a tunnel dug through the mountain from two sides around 1900. However, the two tubes failed. Colonel Barog then committed suicide. A few years later, H.S. Harrington, the chief engineer of the railway, succeeded in digging a tunnel. The unfortunate engineer Barog is still remembered today in the small town by the tunnel with the neat little Barog Station, which resembles a small Scottish station. Some passengers also believe the ghost of Barog still haunts the dark tunnel.

Darjeeling and the narrow gauge railway

Already in 1999, the Darjeeling Himalayan Railway was included in the UNESCO World Heritage List. Built between 1879 and 1881, this friction railway has a gauge of only 610 mm, which is why it is also known as a toy railway in India. It brought relief from the summer heat to colonial officials stationed in Kolkata, the capital of India at the time, and opened up tea-growing areas. Little has changed technically since then, and the trains are still equipped with steam locomotives. The terminus at Darjeeling, a rather modest building, is 2076 m above sea level. The site is dominated by 19th-century British colonial architecture.

The high situated railway station of Ghum

The highest station of the Darjeeling Railway is not the terminus of the Darjeeling, but Ghum (2226 m), where there is also a railway museum at the station. Ghum is often mistakenly referred to in some travel guides as the highest station in the world, sometimes even as the second highest. Both claims are wrong since there are stations at higher altitudes in China since the construction of the Tibet railway (additionally, Peru and Switzerland have higher stations). The highest steam train station, on the other hand, is rather correct, and there is nothing wrong with the designation of India's highest station. In Ghum station, a small, black, house-shaped monument indicates the World Heritage status of the Darjeeling Railway.

The Niligiri Railway

In the south of India, there is a third narrow-gauge railway, the Niligiri Mountain Railway, which has been declared a World Heritage Site by UNESCO. Like the other two, Niligiri is a mountain railway, and like the Darjeeling Railway, it is operated by steam trains. However, with a gauge of 1000 mm, it is not called a "Toy Train" in India. The railway connects the city of Mettupalayam with Udagamandalam in the Nilgiri Mountains of southern India. It is the only rack railway in India. At Coonoor station, a brass plaque with an English text reminds us that the railway was inscribed on the UNESCO World Heritage List in 2005. The terminus Udagamandalam (the town and its station is also called Oatacamund) is characterized by British colonial architecture, like Shimla and Darjeeling. However, both names were too complicated for the British, who once sought relief from the heat of southern India in this "Queen of Hills." They simply called the place "Ooty."

5.4 Pakistan, Bangladesh and Nepal

Pakistan

Lahore and the fort

Lahore station in Pakistan was built by the British colonial masters shortly after the 1857 uprisings. On the silver shovel with which the governor Sir John Lawrence broke the ground was the motto "tam bello quam pace (better peace than war)." But due to the tense situation, the building had to be constructed as a fort at the same time. There were slits in the towers of the station for guns to poke out.

And even today, more than 150 years after the station was built, the situation in Pakistan is anything but relaxed.

Karachi Cantt Station

The name of the most important railway station in the Pakistani metropolis of Karachi, Cantt Station, also refers to the military history of the railway in Pakistan. Cantt stands for "cantonment," and this was the militarily secured suburban area where the station was once located.

Bangladesh

Dhaka Kamalapur and the snake

In both Hinduism and Buddhism of Southern and Southeastern Asia, the snake Naga plays a role. Naga is often depicted as a seven-headed cobra. Although Bangladesh and its capital, Dhaka, are predominantly Muslim, the architecture of the capital's modern Kamalapur station, with its seven supporting elements projecting like cobras on each side, is also compared to a seven-headed snake, i.e., Naga.

Sylhet

A similar railway station, also architecturally impressive because of its special Bangladeshi modernity, is located in the town of Sylhet, which is in the north-eastern tea region of the country. Cube-like building elements are covered by a treetop-like roof. It was built by the architect Rafique Uddin Ahmed in 2004. F.R. Kahn, the engineer responsible for the statics of the Sears Tower in Chicago, also came from Bangladesh.

Sylhet Station

Nepal

Janakpur in Nepal

Katmandu, the capital of Nepal, cannot be reached by train and, therefore, has no railway station. The Janakpur Railway, a 762 mm narrow-gauge railway operated by steam locomotives, is the only railway line in the country. This line is only 29 km long, carries about 1 million passengers per year, and runs from Janakpur Dham to the Indian city of Jaynagar.

Janakpur has only a modest railway station. Yet, despite the low train traffic, there is always a lot going on here. Janakpur has an important Hindu temple complex, and during pilgrimage times, there is a lot of train traffic. The narrow-gauge trains are so crowded that many travellers only find room on the roofs of the trains.

5.5 Sri Lanka

Colombo Fort Station

The Macedonian-born religious sister Mother Teresa (1910-1997) said goodbye to her sister and her mother at Skopje station on 28 September 1928 and boarded the train to Zagreb. She was never to see them again after she arrived in India in 1929. She worked in Kolkata for many decades. Teresa died in September 1997, and in the same year, British director Kevin Connor made a film of her life entitled *Mother Teresa: In the Name of God's Poor*. Yet, the scenes which took place in Kolkata railway station were shot in Fort Station station in Colombo, the capital of Sri Lanka. One reason for the change in location was that it was less hectic and more civilized than the crowded station in Calcutta.

Kandy

Kandy, two and a half hours by train from Colombo, has one of the busiest railway stations in Sri Lanka. The place is an important Buddhist pilgrimage destination since the Buddha's tooth is kept here. In connection with the tooth is the impressive Buddhist procession Esala Perahera, which takes place here every year. It is so colourful that Kandy station's façade has to be washed after the procession every year. However, the station, built in 1857, is so old that a thorough renovation of the building has long been necessary. In 2008, the oil company Chevron finally sponsored a major renovation of Kandy station. The station, which regularly flooded during heavy rainfall— which is not unusual in the mountains—finally got a proper drainage system.

6. The Middle East and the Caucasus

6.1 Middle East

Damascus Hedschas station

The 1050 mm Hedschas Railway was built in 1900-1908 in the Ottoman Empire under the project management of the German engineer Heinrich August Meissner. It once ran from Damascus to Medina. However, an extension of this pilgrim railway to Mecca never came about. The southern portion of the route was soon exposed to Bedouin attacks led by the British Lawrence of Arabia and did not survive for long. The Damascus-Amman route still exists, but it was closed to regular traffic at the end of 2006. A few years earlier, the tracks to the Hegja station in downtown Damascus had been removed for an urban development project. The trains now depart from Cadem station on the outskirts of the city.

Built in a historic oriental style, the Hjjevah station is one of the most beautiful reception buildings in the Middle East. In front of the station is an old German locomotive, and originally, a German architect was also supposed to design a fountain for the station square. The sculpture was supposed to be a lion placing its claw on a Turkish flag.

Medina Hedschas railway station

Medina's Hejja station is surprisingly well preserved, although no trains have arrived here since 1924. Money for restoration work is apparently available in oil-rich Saudi Arabia. Signs at the station indicate construction work. A museum on the history of the Hejaz Railway is being built in the station complex.

The Shah and Tehran Station

Tehran's main railway station was built by German companies and completed in 1939, just before the outbreak of the Second World War. Per the Nazi racial ideology of the time, the Germans saw themselves as Aryans and the Iranians as well. Perhaps this was the reason why the Germans included a swastika in the design of the station ceiling. This was still visible in the station years after the World War. The Shah secretly sympathized with the Germans, but the newly built Transiran Railway became an important supply route for American deliveries to the Soviet Union during the Second World War.

The Shah had his own private station in Tehran's central station. Chairs and the carpet were protected by dust covers, which were only removed when the Shah wanted to travel. Even if he travelled by plane, the royal train had to be made operational to be prepared in case a sudden weather deterioration made a flight impossible. If the Shah was travelling by train, all senior railway staff had to be on stand-by, as all railway department heads had to be on board to give the necessary instructions in the event of any disruption to railway operations.

Baghdad Central Station

The main railway station in Baghdad, Iraq, designed by a British architect and opened in 1953, was looted after the US invasion in 2003 but reopened in 2007 after a $6 million renovation. Yet, the daily train to Mosul was initially used by an average of only ten passengers, almost exclusively by train staff. The Iraqis were simply still too afraid of attacks to be able to travel carefree.

Jerusalem

In the first decades after the founding of Israel, the railway played only a marginal role in the country's transport system. Public transport was and still is dominated by the buses of the Egged Cooperative, the largest bus operator in Israel and the second-largest bus company in the world. A job with Egged was long considered desirable in Israel and resembled a civil servant position for life. Employees of Egged had good chances on the marriage market. However, with the economic upswing in Israel in the last decade, motorized individual transport has increased so much that buses are now also getting stuck in traffic jams. As a result, investment in the rail network, which was poorly developed until that point, has increased. According to the government, railway lines have been built, and a new station, Malha Station, was opened in Jerusalem in 2005. However, because bus transport continues to be very important, another station is now under construction in Jerusalem, directly under the city's central bus station. Additionally, the bus station (and thus the new station) will be connected to a new light rail system (with bullet-proof windows, typical of the country).

Haifa Hashmona railway station

During the 2006 conflict between Israel and Lebanon, a Hezbollah Katyusha missile hit a train yard in Haifa, Israel, killing eight Israeli railway workers. The nearby railway station of Haifa Merkaz Centre was renamed Haifa Merkaz Hashmona Station. Hashmona means "the eight," and this is how the memory of the killed eight railway workers is kept alive.

6.2 Caucasus

Yerevan and the confectioner's style

In 2000, readers of the British magazine *The Independent Traveller* were asked to name their favourite railway station in areas least visited by tourists. David Turns from Liverpool suggested Bled-Jezero Station in Slovenia, Cincinnati Union Station in the US, and Yerevan Central Station in Armenia. Mr. Turns said that the station was a prominent feature of the city since most buildings are not tall due to the risk of earthquakes. The station was built in 1956, making it one of the last Stalinist confectioner's style buildings. The façade, with its colonnades and pointed station tower, completely dominates the station square. Even a now obsolete red star can be seen on the station tower. However, the station, in its well-preserved Soviet splendour, is completely underutilized. When Turns bought his ticket for the train to Tbilisi, he was the only passenger in the station and learned that only four trains depart from it per day.

Gori and Stalin

Gori, Georgia, has a cream yellow, well-preserved neoclassical station with a portico. Until a few years ago, a portrait of Josef Stalin hung, surprisingly, above the station door on the platform side. A statue of Stalin was found in one of the station's waiting areas. The reason for the local appreciation of the Soviet dictator, whose statue also stood in front of Gori town hall until 2010: Stalin was born (1878) in Gori. During the Ossetian conflict in August 2008, Gori was occupied by Russians and South Ossetians. In June 2010, the Georgians removed the statue of Stalin from its pedestal overnight.

The airport station of Tbilisi

Greek mythology tells of a fabulously rich country on the eastern edge of the Black Sea, where Jason and the Argonauts kidnapped the Golden Fleece from King Aeetes with the help of his daughter Medea. The Golden Fleece was the fur of the ram Chrysomeles, who could fly and saved the children of King Athamas from their jealous stepmother in Colchis. The ram was sacrificed, and its fleece hung in a sacred grove where it was guarded by a dragon. Colchis is said to have been what is now Georgia. Georgia was once rich in gold, and sheepskins were used to wash the gold from the rivers, which is probably a basis of the Golden Fleece myth.

Visitors arriving at the airport in the Georgian capital Tbilisi and taking a train to the city centre from the airport station, which former Georgian President Mikheil Saakashvili said was much better than the one in Geneva, may be reminded of this myth. The train station, with its gold-coloured outer cladding and its curved shape with a knob, looks as if someone had tied a knot in the Golden Fleece and thrown it over the train station.

Sukhumi

Photoblogs on the internet contain pictures showing the morbid charm of a decaying Abkhazia Railway Station overgrown by nature. This is the railway station of Sukhumi, the capital of the Abkhazia province, which has broken away from Georgia. In Soviet times, Sukhumi was an important seaside resort with a representative railway station. However, the civil war and the closing of the border brought the railway traffic to a standstill, and the station fell into disuse.

7. Turkey

Turkey has a relatively extensive railway network, many of which was built later than in Europe. Nevertheless, the country's railway history is interesting because various European powers have left their mark on it. In the 19th century, the Ottoman Empire, which was characterized by a stagnating oriental society, fell further and further behind the modernizing Western European powers. During the Crimean War, it was already considered the "sick man of Europe." Typical of the "Orient," the area of present-day Turkey was also characterized by a feudalistic rent-seeking capitalist system, which allowed profits to be consumed by urban landowners and inhibited entrepreneurial initiative, investment, and innovation. Turkish entrepreneurship did not develop in this way, not even in the railway sector. But soon, foreign companies stepped in to develop economic potential. A British company built Turkey's first railway line to transport the cotton grown there to England. Meanwhile, French companies took care of the Black Sea region and the coal there, and a Belgian company opened the railway station in Bursa. The Turkish word for railway station, Gar, is derived from the French word "gare." A little later, the Germans also played an important role. German architects built the two termini in Istanbul—Deutsche Bank financed one of them—and beginning in 1903, the Germans built the Baghdad Railway from Konya to the Iraqi capital. Later, German exiles influenced Ankara's urban planning, including a Bauhaus-style central station. The German influence can still be seen today in the fact that the departure of the train is authorized by the staff at the platform with the word "Fertik."

Map of Turkey's Railroad Network

(Source: Wikipedia, own work by Maximilian Dörrbecker, CC-BY SA 2.5)

7.1 Izmir and Southern Aegean

Aydin

Turkey's first railway line was opened in 1856, was 130 km long, and ran from Izmir to Aydin. This is explained by the cotton grown in the province of Aydin, which was in great demand by the British textile industry. Sometimes, even the American Civil War is mentioned, which is said to have caused cotton supply shortages, but this did not take place until 1861-1865. In any case, cotton growing in the Aydin area was economically relevant enough to persuade the British Levant Company to build a railway line. Aydin, by the way, is situated on the meander that has become a byword for meandering rivers. Aydin still has a railway station today, but it is architecturally rather unimpressive and has little traffic.

Izmir Alsançak

The Alsançak railway station of Izmir, built in 1858 and not far from the port, is today the oldest railway station in Turkey. In May 2006, the station was closed due to the extension of the Izmir Metro and was used for concerts, among other things. On 19 May 2010, it was reopened for passenger transport as an IZBAN suburban railway station.

Izmir Basmane

Basmane is today the main railway station in the city of Izmir. However, even here, there is no brisk train traffic since the railway network in Turkey is not very well developed and buses dominate the long-distance traffic. At least the station has an underground station (the small underground network of Izmir consists of only one line). At night, the station's facade is bathed in blue light. The reasons for this are similar to those in Western Europe: it discourages people to take drugs since the blue light prevents them from finding their veins.

Camlik and the steam locomotive museum

Between Aydin and Izmir is the railway station of the village Camlik. Here, Atatürk had his headquarters in his White Train during the Aegean campaign. Today, the Turkish Railway Museum is located on the railway station grounds. Many steam locomotives, which were still in service in Western Turkey until the 1980s, are parked here.

Dalaman station without rails

Dalaman, a holiday resort not far from Marmaris in south-western Turkey, is known for its low-cost airport. Another of the town's attractions is a "railway station" that never had rail transport. The Egyptian governor Padischa Abbas was an enthusiastic hunter and wanted to have a hunting lodge in Dalaman, which is rich with game. A French company was awarded the building contract in 1905. At the same time, they were also commissioned to design a railway station building for a station near Alexandria in Egypt. The French confused the two projects; the hunting lodge plans were sent to Egypt, and the station plans to Dalaman. No one noticed the confusion, and therefore, a station building was built in a city without rail traffic. Some sources even claim that tracks were laid. Today, the station is the seat of the local agricultural administration.

Istanbul-Sirkeci - Orient in Europe

The Sirkeci station, located on the European side, was once famous as the terminus of the Orient Express. In the twenties, a goods train brought clothes from France to Turkey every week. Kemal Atatürk wanted to introduce his countrymen to the western style of clothing. The reception building of the station, opened in 1890, has an oriental feel to it. This is no surprise considering that the architect was the Prussian August Jachmund, who was sent to Istanbul by the German government to study oriental architecture.

In 1963, a scene from the James Bond film *From Russia with Love* was shot in the railway station. Several thousand onlookers crowded into the station. At times, the onlookers had to be distracted by a stunt so as not to disturb the filming.

Istanbul-Haydarpasa - Europe in Asia

The Haydarpasa station on the Asian side looks more European. This should come as no surprise, as it was built by the Philipp Holzmann company according to plans of the German architects' Otto Ritter and Helmut Cuno. The castle-like station in the neo-Renaissance style was a gift from Kaiser Wilhelm II to Sultan Abdülhamid and allied Turkey. 1100 piles, each 21 metres long, had to be driven into the ground to create a stable foundation. The station is one of the few in the world to be surrounded by water on three sides. In 1979, the station was damaged by an oil tanker fire but was repaired. In November 2010, the roof and the fourth floor were destroyed by fire.

Karaagaç and the first bomber

During the First Balkan War (October 1912 - May 1913), Serbia, Montenegro, Bulgaria, and Greece fought against the Ottoman Empire. A Bulgarian pilot dropped the first aerial bomb in a war (making him the first bomber pilot in history) at the Turkish railway station of Karaagaç near Edirne.

Karaagaç is located on the western bank of the river Evros (Turkish: Meric), and the river later formed the border with Bulgaria and then Greece. Karaagaç remained as a suburb of Edirne, but a new railway station had to be built east of the river, as the old Karaagaç station was cut off from the rest of the country by the border. The old station, which has been restored in the meantime, now houses a university, and a restaurant has been established in the steam train on the tracks.

Izmit and the stonemasons

Germans, English, French, and even Belgians have played an important role in the development of the Turkish railway network. But what about the Italians? When the reception building of Izmit station was built, Italian stonemasons were at least working on the façade. After a new railway station was built on the outskirts of the city, the historic station of Izmit became a restaurant. In front of the station, there are still tracks with a steam locomotive, which reminds of old times.

When Atatürk died in November 1938, his body was transported by ship from Dolmus Palace to Izmit. From there, a special train, which stopped at many stops to give the people the opportunity to say goodbye to him, continued its journey to Ankara.

The number on the station roof

On the roof of Ankara's central station, a number in neon-illuminated digits can be seen, which is changed every year. The letters TCDD precede the number, and Yil is written after it. What is it all about? TCDD is the Turkish State Railway Company, Yil means years, and the number indicates the years that have passed since 1856, the year in which the first railway ran in Turkey. Therefore, in 2020, one can read "TCDD: 164 years," although TCDD itself has only existed since 1927.

Ankara Central Station - Atatürk's first home

Kemal Atatürk, the father of modern Turkey, resided in the stationmaster's house at Platform 1 after he arrived in the new capital Ankara in 1919-1921. At Platform 1, there was a telegraph station, which Atatürk used extensively to keep his country together. Atatürk's German-made railway carriage, a gift from Adolf Hitler, had special antennas for telegraph traffic and can be viewed in the station.

Gazi and Atatürk's model plants

In Gazi near Ankara, Atatürk had model farms set up to familiarize Turks with modern agriculture. A small railway station was built to make the journey easier. In his last years, Atatürk got off the train more and more often in this small but nice station instead of Ankara's main station. Today, Gazi is an urban railway station in Ankara. The station building was restored true to the original in 2000 and now houses a restaurant. It is possible to visit all rooms.

Behiç Erkin's grave in Eskisehir station

Behiç Erkin (1876-1961) was the first director-general of the predecessor organization of the Turkish state railway company TCDD, which was founded in 1927. During the Turkish War of Liberation (1919-1923), Erkin took control and nationalized the railways, which were then still in foreign hands, at the central railway junction at Eskisehir. When family names became compulsory for Turkish citizens in 1934, Kemal Atatürk gave the family name Erkin, meaning independent, to Behiç. After 1928, Erkin worked as a diplomat, and from 1939, he was the Turkish diplomat to France. In Paris, he issued papers to Turkish citizens of Jewish origin, and he was very generous in his efforts, ensuring that more than 18,000 Jews remained safe, some of whom were able to leave for Turkey. Behiç Erkin is, therefore, considered a kind of "Turkish smuggler." Erkin died in Istanbul in 1961 and, following his wish to be a railwayman, which had remained dear to his heart, he was buried in the Eskisehir railway station.

Ismet Pasha and the railway station of Inönü

In the Greek-Turkish War, the battle of Inönü took place in January 1921. The Turkish troops had entrenched themselves at Inönü station, not far from Eskisehir. The commander of the Turkish Western Front, Ismet Pasha, later gave himself the surname Inönü in memory of these events. He became the second president of Turkey after the death of Atatürk in 1938.

The meeting in Yenice

In January 1943, a secret meeting between British Prime Minister Churchill and Turkish President Ismet Inönü took place in a railway carriage in a remote station near Adana.

Churchill wanted to persuade Turkey to enter the war against Germany and open a second front in the Balkans. Inönü, however, did not want to be drawn into the war and maintained Turkey's neutral position. Therefore, Churchill left empty-handed. A group of young boarding school students in a waiting train in a station got wind of the important meeting. The student Sudi Abac was particularly impressed, also by the attitude of his state president. Many years later, he set out to find the missing railway carriage, but it was not until the 1990s that he was able to track it down. He had the wagon restored and brought to the Peace Park in Yenice, where it can still be seen today. Photographs in the Yenice railway station remind us of the meeting of the two statesmen.

Afyonkarahisar

Afyon is the Turkish word for opium. The Afyon province in Western Turkey and its capital, which is an important railway junction in Western Anatolia, were given this name due to the poppy that was grown in the area. But since opium is not a good name for a city, the Turkish parliament officially renamed the place Afyonkarahisar (Opium Black Castle) in 2004. They did not want to have a sign saying "Opium" on the station building either, so they named the station after Turkey's first Minister of Transport, Ali Cetinkaya, who rendered outstanding services to the railway and had more than 1000 km of railway lines built.

From Burdur to Antalya

Turkey has a topography which is unfavourable to railway construction, with mountain ranges running in an undulating west-east direction, forcing the railway to make detours. Because of the turbulent topography, there is no railway line running along the Black Sea coast or Lake Van.

Since a large part of the railway network was only built when an alternative mode of transport was already available in the form of motorized road traffic, connections that were planned but were topographically difficult and, therefore, expensive were ultimately no longer realized. These include the connection of the isolated route Eregli-Amutcuk on the Black Sea with Zonguldak or the planned line from Burdur in the Anatolian highlands to Antalya, 900 metres below, on the Mediterranean Sea. Antalya was a relatively small city at the time of the Turkish railway construction and had only 28,000 inhabitants in 1950. But with the growing holiday traffic, the population was to double with every decade thereafter. The city's airport, which proved to be more important for its development than a railway station, also contributed to this. Today Antalya has about 800,000 inhabitants. It is a city of almost a million people without a railway station. However, there has been rail traffic in the city since 1997. A tram system has been established, which is operated with second-hand tram vehicles purchased from Nuremberg. Today, Burdur itself is connected to the Turkish railway network by a branch line. In 1973, a stone with an inscription was brought to the English archaeologist Stephen Mitchell, which had been found at Burdur station. It turned out to be an edict of the Roman Emperor Tiberius from 15 AD, which regulated the transport through the area of the ancient city of Sagalassos near Burdur.

7.4 Bursa area

Mudanya and the hotel

Until 1948, there was a rail connection from the port of Mudanya on the Marmara Sea—where ships from Istanbul arrived—to Bursa, once the capital of the Ottoman Empire. The Ottoman government first tried to build the line on its own without having to grant concessions to foreign companies. However, due to a lack of capital, the project was taken over in 1874 by French contractors, who completed the railway line within a year. However, the railway could not be opened because British locomotives were delivered with the wrong gauge. In January 1891, the Belgian travel entrepreneur George Nagelmackers—who also initiated the railway line which later became known as the Orient Express—bought the line for £27,000, founded the Chemin de Fer de Moudania-Brousse (Bursa), and had the track gauge changed to 1000mm. Yet, the line was hardly profitable, as Bursa was not connected to the rest of the railway network. In 1932, the state railway company TCDD took over the line but closed it down only 16 years later. Mudanya station, which used to be a transfer station for ships, is now a middle-class hotel with a good view of the Marmara Sea.

Bursa Acemler

Bursa (the former capital of the Ottoman Empire) and Antalya are now two major Turkish cities without rail connections. Bursa once had a railway station and now has a light rail system, while Antalya never had a railway station. For the Bursa Acemler station, the website of the Ministry of Culture and Tourism of Turkey reports the following anecdote. When the Belgian Chemin de Fer de Moudania-Brousse opened the Bursa Acemler station in

1892, the timetable on the notice board showed hours that were common in Western European timekeeping. At that time, however, Turkey had its own system of timekeeping in which day and night were divided into 12 hours each, the length of which varied according to the season. In September 1892, the railway company, therefore, put up a notice to inform passengers that the timetables were based on Western European hours. In the end, however, it was necessary to give in to the habits of the local population and to change the timetable to times in Turkish hours.

The orphan girl in Bursa railway station

In 1925, an orphan girl named Sabiha asked Atatürk if he could help her get into boarding school upon his arrival in Bursa. On 22 September 1925, the child-friendly Atatürk (he supposedly said that "Children are a new beginning and a new future") adopted Sabiha. In 1934, surnames became mandatory in Turkey, and Sabiha was called Gökcen (which means "belonging to heaven"). Sabiha was allowed to live with his three other adoptive daughters in his residence in Ankara. Later, the girls attended university in Istanbul. In 1935, when Turkey's first flight school opened, Sabiha showed enthusiasm for aviation and was allowed to go to Moscow, along with seven male students, to learn how to fly. In 1936, she went to the Turkish Air Force Academy. In 1937, she took part in a military operation and became the first fighter pilot, world-wide. She flew during the Korean War and was nicknamed "Amazon of the Skies." When the United States Air Force, published a poster titled "The 20 Greatest Aviators of History" in 1996, Gökcen was depicted as the only woman on it. Sabiha Gokcen died on 22 March 2001: her 88th Birthday. That same year, Istanbul´s second airport, located on the Asian side (the airport in the European part is called Atatürk Airport), was named after Sabiha Gökcen.

Balikeshir and the four languages

Arabic characters can be seen at the reception building of Balikeshir station. This is a remnant from the early days of the Turkish railway. In the Ottoman Empire, Arabic letters were used, but it was Atatürk who had the country convert to a Latin based system in 1928. But even then, the station signs Arabic, which represented the French version of the city name, remained. After all, French was the international lingua franca at that time. This can still be seen in the Turkish word "gar," which is derived from the French word "gare," meaning railway station (another word for station is "tren istasyonu," from the English word train station), and so the letters Balikesir Gar are still found on the station façade of the town. In Balikesir, with the recent renovation of the station, another language has been added: English. Information boards in Turkish and English show the way to the ticket office and the waiting area.

7.5 Black Sea coast

Zonguldak and the coal

The station sign at Zonguldak shows French language influence twice. Besides the word "Gar" for train station, the name of the town itself is French-influenced. Two monuments in the city show the reason. In the city centre of Zonguldak, there is a monument on which rails can be seen. However, it does not represent a railway station, but a coal mine. Another monument in the town shows Uzun Mehmet, who first found coal in the area. Mehmet travelled by ship to Istanbul in 1829 to show his discovery. He received a lifelong pension from the government in recognition of his discovery, but he was murdered soon after. In 1835, Croatian miners, sent by the Austrian government, started to mine coal in Zonguldak. French and Belgian mining companies were also active here, and they named the town after the local Göldagi mountain, Geul-Dagh, which later became Zonguldak. To connect this coal area with the hinterland, a railway line was built to Inner Anatolia. Not far from Zonguldak, the railway line led to the development of Karabük, the centre of the Turkish steel industry.

Samsun-Carşamba

In 1924, the tobacco baron family Zade received a 75 -year concession from the Turkish state to build a 750 mm narrow-gauge railway on the Black Sea from Alacam via Samsun to Terme. However, only the Samsun-Carşamba section was later realized. On Tuesday, 21 September 1924, Atatürk broke the ground with a silver shovel. Actually, he should have waited a day because Carşamba, the terminus of the route, is the Turkish word for Wednesday. With the world economic crisis in 1929, the tobacco barons got into economic difficulties, and the state had to take over the line, which originally opened in 1926. This 37 km long railway line was at times the last narrow-gauge line of the Turkish Railways. It was closed down in 1971.

Batman

The railway station in the eastern Turkish town of Batman is nothing special but seeing the sign saying "Batman" will make you smile.

Here, in the Kurdish populated east, names are sometimes a political issue. When the Kurdish mayor Hüseyin Kalkan wanted to have streets in the city named after freedom fighters such as Mahatma Gandhi, the central government refused to do so since it saw these changes as them hidden Kurdish efforts for autonomy. Kalkan himself later led a campaign against a name. In spring 2009, he wanted to file a lawsuit against the British director Christopher Nolan, whom he accused of having illegally used the name of his city in the Batman film *The Dark Night*. By the way, the city was originally called Iluh when it was founded in 1938. Only one year later, the comic hero Batman was born. In 1942, the town got a railway connection, and the name Iluh was written on the station sign. In 1943, the first Batman movie was released. It was not until oil was found in the 1950s that the little nest grew into a real town, which was renamed Batman in 1957, after the local river.

Kars - the Russian railway station

The city of Kars is located in the very east of Turkey, not far from the border with Armenia. Years prior, this was the border to the Russian Empire. Kars had a fortress that withstood several sieges. Yet, in 1828, it was stormed by the Russians for the first time. In the Crimean War of 1855, the Russians forced Kars to surrender again. After Kars was again conquered by the Russians in the Russian-Turkish War of 1877-78, the Turks had to cede Kars to Russia in the Treaty of San Stefano. In the years that followed, Kars took on a Russian architectural character with Orthodox churches, straight-lined street blocks, and a railway station that could have stood in the style of a larger Russian provincial town. Yet, in 1918, Russia lost Kars to the Turks again with the Peace of Brest-Litovsk. In the following years, the traces of the Russian decades were gradually erased; Orthodox churches became mosques, and finally, in the 1970s, the railway station built by the Russians was demolished and replaced by a modern Turkish building. As the railway line from Kars to Armenia has been closed since 1990 for political reasons, there is now a project for a new railway line, the Kars-Tbilisi-Baku Railway, which is to connect eastern Turkey via Georgia with oil-rich Azerbaijan. Construction of the new railway line has already started.

Malatya and the Art Deco Design

In the eastern Turkish city of Malatya, there is a surprisingly stylish Art Deco station. It was built in 1931 by the Danish company Nyquist & Holm (Nohab) during the construction of a railway line from Fevzipasa to Diyarbakir. Although the station's design fit the fashion of the time of its construction, it did not necessarily fit in with local building traditions.

Tatvan and Van

The topography around Lake Van in eastern Turkey is so difficult that no tracks have been laid at all. Long-distance trains to Tehran run to Tatvan on the western shore of the lake. There, you change to a ferry and continue by train in Van on the eastern shore. Due to the low train frequency, there are no concrete plans for a railway line along the lakeshore.

8. Siberia and Central Asia

Nureyev's birth

The birthplace of dancer Rudolf Nureyev (1938-1993) is sometimes referred to as Irkutsk, but this is only an approximation. Nureyev's very pregnant Tartar mother wanted to be with her husband at birth, who was stationed in Vladivostok as an officer of the Red Army. Therefore, she set off for the Pacific on the Trans-Siberian Railway. However, on the train, the contractions began. Nureyev, considered the greatest dancer of the 20th century, was born (17 March 1938) on the train before the station of Irkutsk was even reached.

Yekaterinburg

Ekaterinburg (Sverdlovsk, 1924-1991) is situated on the eastern side of the Ural Mountains, only 40 km from the Europe-Asia dividing line in the Urals. The bridge between Asia and Europe can also be seen in the railway station, where two allegorical figures depict Europe and Asia.

Yekaterinburg-Shartash

In the summer of 1918, the Russian royal family arrived at Shartash train station in Yekaterinburg from their place of exile: Tobolsk. The Bolsheviks wanted to avoid meeting the Czar at the main station because they wanted to settle things discreetly. On 17 July 1918, Tsar Nicholas II and his family were shot and killed, allegedly on the orders of Lenin.

Novosibirsk

Built in the 1930s, the station of Novosibirsk is the largest of the Trans-Siberian Railway. That fact that steam locomotives were still used at the time of construction becomes evident in the facade. The station building looks like the profile of a steam locomotive. Novosibirsk, Russia's third-largest city today, was founded in 1893 and was known until 1925 as Novonikolayevsk, named after the last Tsar.

Sludyanka - the marble railway station

The Sludyanka station of the Trans-Siberian railway is the only station in the world built of marble. Therefore, it got the nickname marble station. Near the town, there is a marble quarry. This marble is mainly used for gravestones. With the marble station, the state wanted to celebrate the progress of the construction of the Trans-Siberian railway. By the way, all stations on the Trans-Siberian railway show Moscow time on the station clock to help passengers gain a reference time.

Birobidzhan

In 1928, a Jewish Autonomous Region was established in the eastern Soviet Union on the border with China. By creating a "Soviet Zion," Stalin pursued various strategic objectives, such as creating a buffer zone with China, the exploitation of raw materials, and the economic development of the sparsely populated area. It was planned that within ten years 150,000 Jews would be settled. But these numbers were never reached, and after the collapse of the Soviet Union, many of the Jewish inhabitants emigrated to Israel, Germany, and North America.

The capital was Birobidzhan, which was reached in 1898 by the Trans-Siberian Railway. Its station is the only one in the world that shows the city name in Cyrillic and Hebrew characters.

Vladivostok

Since 1903, the Trans-Siberian Railway has connected the Pacific city of Vladivostok with Moscow, which is 9288 km away. Vladivostok station is considered a copy of the Yaroslavl station in Moscow, built by Fyodor Schechtel from 1902 to 1904. After the Russian Revolution, the Communists took the opportunity to saw off the heads of the double-headed eagle on the façade of Vladivostok station.

Vladivostok station is the starting point of the Trans-Siberian Railway. The cities name means "rule the east (Vlad-ruler, vostok-east." However, Vladivostok is not, as one might think, the easternmost station of the Trans-Siberian railway, but the southernmost. The easternmost station is the city of Khabarovsk, named after the Cossack Khabarov.

Nakhodka

During the Cold War, Vladivostok was off-limits to foreigners. The ferries to Japan departed from the second endpoint of the Trans-Siberian route: the port of Nakhodka. The American writer Paul Theroux said in his 1975 travel book *The Great Railway Bazaar* that Nakhodka train station had stucco walls and the dimensions of the madhouse in Kabul.

Tashkent and the Uzbek Express

German director Veit Helmer (*1968) shot the short film *Uzbek-Express* (a video can be found on YouTube) in 2001, in cooperation with the Goethe Institute in Tashkent (Uzbek: Toshkent) and the local film school students, at the city's main railway station. Back then, the station, built after the devastating earthquake of 1966, still had a lot of Soviet flair. However, after a renovation in 2007, the station's name now appears in Latin Uzbek letters instead of Cyrillic.

Gila

Uzbek journalist Hamit Ismailov (*1954) wrote the novel *The Railway* in 1997, which was translated into English in 2006. The novel focuses on the railway station of the fictitious Uzbek small town of Gila, In the novel, the fate of the during the 20th century is revealed. At times, the railway station serves in the novel as the communist party headquarters of the town.

Bishkek and Frunze

A Frunze monument stands in front of the railway station in Bishkek, the capital of Kyrgyzstan. Mikhail Vasilievich Frunze was a commander in the Russian Civil War. He was the son of a Romanian farmer from Bessarabia and was born in Bishkek in 1885. He died in 1925 during a stomach operation, and there is a rumour that Stalin had a hand in the death of this potential rival. When the Soviet Republic of Kyrgyzstan was founded in 1926, its capital was renamed Frunze. Since 1991, however, the city and its railway station have again been called Bishkek. Frunze's monument still stands in front of the station.

9. Oceania

The Australian railway network has not been planned uniformly. There are three gauges: 1067mm narrow gauge (Cape Gauge), standard gauge, and 1600mm wide gauge. Most of the railways in Australia are state-owned. However, because the country is rich in raw materials and distances are long, railways play an important role in freight transport. Freight transport finances the infrastructure, so there is even more regular long-distance passenger traffic, even on routes such as Adelaide-Perth (with few trains, however, since the number of passengers is rather low). However, in urban areas such as Sydney and Melbourne, where local rail transport has the function of an underground with underground inner-city lines, it is of considerable importance. In cities such as Perth and Brisbane, local rail transport is also growing through the expansion of the network. Thanks to the well-functioning local transport system, the volume of rail traffic is around 400 million people per year.

In New Zealand, actually a railway country in terms of distances, only the conurbations of Auckland and Wellington have significant rail passenger traffic due to the country's low population density. Additionally, few long-distance routes have survived the privatization of the railways. These remaining lines are mainly used for tourism. New Zealand's railways transport only about 10 million passengers per year.

At the beginning of the 20th century, the most important cities of the country tried to outdo each other with spectacular railway station buildings, which led to interesting railway station architecture.

Melbourne Flinders Street Station

Melbourne, the capital of the state of Victoria, has a relatively European character. While road traffic dominates in many other cities in the southern hemisphere, rail traffic still plays an important role in Melbourne. Three-quarters of the operated tram lines in the southern hemisphere are in this city (343 km). Melbourne's central station building, Flinders Street Station, which was built between 1905 and 1910, is still of considerable importance for suburban traffic. The station is considered the busiest in the southern hemisphere, with 1500 trains per working day (other stations have more passengers). Platform 1 is 708 metres long, making it the fourth-longest in the world. The station building is also an important landmark and a popular meeting place for locals, who say, "I'll meet you under the clocks." This refers to a row of clocks above the main entrance, showing the departure times of the main lines. When the clocks were replaced by digital ones during a renovation of the station, an outcry went through the tradition-conscious city. The old analog clocks were then quickly reinstalled.

Melbourne Batman

The city of Melbourne was once almost called Batmania because it was founded by farmer John Batman. Batman went down in history by concluding a contract with the Aborigines for the use of land, which was different from the usual practice at the time. Batman leased the area of today's Melbourne from the Aborigines for 40 blankets, 30 axes, 100 knives, 50 scissors, 100 pounds of flour, and 6 shirts. He then called the area Batmania. However, this name did not become established for the later city. Nevertheless, a station was later named after him in Melbourne, the Batman Station, which still exists today. By the way, there is a city called Batman (with a station) in the eastern Turkey.

Melbourne Southern Cross

Melbourne's new Southern Cross Station (formerly Spencer Street Station) was opened in 2006 for the Commonwealth Games. Its architecture was awarded the Lubetkin Prize for the most extraordinary building outside Europe by the Royal Institute of British Architects in 2007.

Sydney Central

Like Melbourne, Sydney does not have an underground but has an extensive suburban rail network that runs underground in the city centre (like suburban trains in German cities), partially replacing the non-existent underground. Sydney Central Station, built in 1906, with its 75-metre high neo-Gothic bell tower, is a source of pride to the people of Sydney. However, the station holds a dark secret: it was built on the site of a cemetery. The dead were exhumed in 1901 to make room for the station.

Sydney Redfern

The first railway station in Sydney was opened in the Redfern district as early as 1855. There is still a Redfern Station today. Because it is only a few kilometres from the terminus Sydney Central, the Australian expression "getting off at Redfern" is used as a paraphrase for Coitus Interruptus.

Rookwood Cemetary Station N°1

Seventeen km from the centre of Sydney lies the large Rookwood Cemetery, the largest multi-religious burial site in the southern hemisphere. A railway line passes by the cemetery, and once. there were even three cemetery stations which were connected to Sydney by regular cemetery trains. The most prominent of them, the neo-Gothic Haslem's Creek Cemetery Station - later called Necropolis and finally, Cemetery Station N° 1 - was closed in 1948 and rebuilt in the Australian capital Canberra in 1958 as All Saints' Church.

The modest Canberra station

Sydney and Melbourne are considered to be great urban rivals. As both cities once claimed the function of capital, a new capital location between the two cities was chosen as a compromise. This new capital Canberra was supposed to be quite modest. This is also evident in Canberra's Kingston station, which has the appearance of an inconspicuous suburban station.

Port Pirie

One of Australia's most architecturally striking railway stations is located in the South Australian town of Port Pirie. Port Pirie has become prosperous because of its mineral resources, and the town is home to the world's largest lead smelter. Port Pirie is crossed by a central east-west railway axis of Australia so that many goods trains pass through the town. In order to avoid having to make a fuss in the old station, a rail connection was built on the outskirts of the town, so that the old Piries station lost its railway function. It now houses an art museum.

Alice Springs and The Ghan

From 1929 to 1980, Alice Springs, located in the heart of the Australian continent, could only be reached by a narrow gauge line (1067 mm). Today, a museum reminds of the old trains. The museum is located in a station that was built especially for this purpose. The blueprints for a station that was supposed to be built in Alice Springs in 1930 were used. There is also a rock on the railway site, which is associated with an Aboriginal legend of a dog-man. When older Aborigines rub against it, it is said to make the dogs howl and excited. In 2004, the railway line from Adelaide to Alice Springs was extended to Darwin on the north coast.

The passenger trains that travel on this line are called "The Ghan." The name is derived from "Afghanistan-Express," a nod to the Afghan camel drivers who used to provide transport in the hot outback of Australia.

The train station of Cook

In 1917, during the construction of the Trans-Australian Railway from Perth to Adelaide, the town of Cook and its railway station were built on the desert-like Nullarbor Plain (so named because there are no trees). One of the functions of the station was to provide water for steam locomotives. When the Australian railways were privatized in 1997, they no longer needed this railway town. However, the station still serves as a diesel filling station for railway vehicles, and there are still accommodation facilities for locomotive drivers.

At 478 km, the Nullarbor Plain is the longest completely straight railway line in the world.

9.2 New Zealand

The Britomart Transport Centre

In downtown Auckland, on Queen Street, there is a monumental historic post office building. Right next door and not far from the ferries was once the city's railway station. In 1930, the station function was moved to an area where space was more generous. However, in July 2003, the train returned, this time, the tracks were moved under the post office building, and the latter became a terminus station, the Britomart Transport Centre. However, Auckland's rail service is not electrified, so Britomart is one of the few underground stations served by diesel trains.

The "American Embassy"

Auckland Central Station, built in 1930 on reclaimed land, is one of New Zealand's most self-assured monumental public buildings from the first half of the 20th century. It was designed by William Henry Gummer (1884-1966), a student of the famous English architect Sir Edward Lutyens. Lutyens was also responsible for the monumental colonial architecture of New Delhi. In 2003, the main station was moved to the Britomart Transport Centre, which is located in a former post office building, and the station was converted into a dormitory for the University of Auckland. As the building is home to a large number of US students, it is now known as the American Embassy. Somehow, the former reception building should look familiar to American students. The station was modeled on the Union Station in the US capital Washington.

Wellington's large railway station

After Auckland's self-confident station building made its mark architecturally in 1930, New Zealand's capital was not allowed to be lousy. When the neo-Georgian station building at Wellington Station was opened in 1937 on land reclaimed from the sea, it was New Zealand's largest building. No less than 1,750,000 bricks and 1500 tons of granite and marble were used in the station. The Fletcher Building company won its first major contract with the station and later became one of the largest companies in the country.

Dunedin - the gingerbread station

Dunedin Station on New Zealand's South Island was opened in 1906 and is one of the most striking station buildings in the oceanic region. In the Flemish medieval style, resembling a cloth hall with a belfry, the brown façade, bordered by white elements, was so reminiscent of a particular pastry that the architect George A. Troup came up with the nickname "Gingerbread George." The station now houses a restaurant, a museum, and the offices of a tourist railway, whose trains run from the station to a nearby gorge. Like the (coastal) stations of Wellington and Auckland, it was built on reclaimed land.

A gingerbread station at the (other) end of the world!

Dunedin Station (Picture: Antilived, Wikipedia

Annex

1. Remarkable/most beautiful stations

Featuring in various lists of top stations

Station/ Source	1	2	3	4	5	6	Summe
New York Grand Central	x		x	x	x	x	5
London St. Pancras	x	(x)		x	x		4
Bombay CST*		x	x		x	x	4
Helsinki Main Station	x	x		x			3
Antwerpen CS		x			x		2
Lahore (Pakistan)	x				x		2
Milano Centrale				x		x	2
Washington Union Station				x			1
Los Angeles Union Station			x				1
Philadelphia Gravers Lane		x					1
Toronto Union Station			x				1
Buenos Aires Retiro		x					1
London Paddington		(x)					1
Santa Maria N, Florenz	x						1
Dublin Heuston Station				x			1
Leipzig Hbf				x			1
Limoges Bénédictins					x		1
Madrid Atocha					x		1
Wladiwostok			x				1
Melbourne Flinders Street		x					1
Maputo Hbf (Mosambique)					x		1
Kuala Lumpur Station		x					1
Hua Hin (Thailand)					x		1

Bold: on several lists, ( ) Parts of the station * UNESCO world heritage

1. J. Glancey in *The Guardian* of 23. 11. 2006 (6 stations)
2. Mark Irving `*1001 Buildings you must see before you die´*, Cassel Illustrated, London 2007
3. Richard Cavendish (Editor) `*1001 Historic Sites you must see before you die´*, Cassel Illustrated, London 2007
4. Brian Solomon `Railway masterpieces´, 2002
5. Newsweek 19 January 2009, Routes, List of 9 best stations
6. Other Lists: UNESCO-World heritage: Bombay CST
   The US-architect Frank Lloyd Wright counted Milano Centrale and New York Grand Central amongst the most beautiful stations

2. Models for stations

Station	Model *(partly)*
Asia	
Bombay CST (Victoria Terminus)	Neogothic style partially inspired by St. Pancras/London
Da Lat (Vietnam)	Deauville (France)
Hsinchu (Taiwan)	Old station of Heidelberg?
Seoul	Tokyo Station
Tokyo (Main) Station	Amsterdam CS
Wladiwostok Bahnhof	Jaroslawl- Station Moscow
Africa	
Pointe Noire (Kongo)	Deauville (little similarity)

Statues/Plaques/Pictures in/at Stations

Station	Statue/Plaque/Picture
China	
Shaoshan	Mao Tsetung-Portrait
Shenyang	Sun bird (Symbol of Shenyang)
Zhangjiakou	Zhan Tianyou (Railway engineer)
Qinglongqiao	Zhan Tianyou (Railway engineer)
Japan	
Tokio-Ebisu	Ebisu-Good of luck
Tokio-Kamiigusa	Gundam-Robot (Manga-Heroe)
T.-Hamamatsucho	Manneken Pis (Platform)
Tokio-Yurakucho	Rackoon (Platform)
Other countries	
Gori (Georgia)	Stalin (born in Gori), Picture+Statue
Chabarowsk (Rus.)	Chabarow (cossack discoverer)
Bishkek (Kirg.)	Frunse (Russian general)
Pyöngyang (Korea)	Kim Il Sung Portrait (in all stations)
Choir (Mongolia)	Kosmonaut Gürragchaa
Yenice (Turkey)	Picture of the meetingChurchill-Inönü

3. Rail traffic in Asian and African countries

2009	Network length (km)	Passengers (million)	Pass.-km (billion)	Tonn-km (billion)
China	139 000	3660	1471	3008
India	68 155	8116 (17)	1150 (17)	691 (18)
Japan	27 311	9392 (16)*	432 (16)	21 (14)
S. Korea	4 165	1020 (09)	77.8 (16)	10.6 (06)
Pakistan	8 100	52.4 (18)	20.3 (15)	5.9 (06)
Indonesia	6 000	393 (18)	25.7 (17)	4.4 (07)
Kazakhstan	15 530	22-9 (18)	19.2 (17)	236 (12)
Iran	16 998	28 (18)	13.3 (17)	22 (13)
Taiwan	1 782	292 (18)	19.8 (15)	1.0 (07)
Thailand	4 900	50 (17)	8.0 (11)	3 (11)
Turkey	12 740	101 (18)	5.4	11 (14)
Vietnam	3 364	11 (02)	4.7 (07)	4 (12)
Bangladesh	2 835	78 (18)	10.0 (17)	0.8 (06)
Sri Lanka	1508	139 (17)	4.8 (07)	0.14 (07)
Egypt	7024	550 (18)	40.8 (08)	2 (10)
Algeria	4 440	39 (18)	1.55 (17)	1.0 (17)
Morocco	2 109	35 (18)	4.5 (18)	4.1 (09)
S. Africa	26 000	269 (17)	13.9 (07)	135 (14)
Tunisia	2 165	41 (17)	1.2 (17)	2 (10)

Source: Wikipedia, World Bank, * Japan all railways: 25 bn passengers

Literature

Les plus belles histoires des trains
Timée Editions, Boulogne 2003

Bund Deutscher Architekten (Hrsg.)
Renaissance der Bahnhöfe
Vieweg Verlag, Braunschweig 1996

Harri Czepeck
Eisenbahnen in Afrika
Verlag für Verkehrswesen, Berlin 1990

Mark Irving
1001 Buildings You Must See Before You Die
Cassel Illustrated, London 2007

Lis Künzli (Hrsg.)
Bahnhöfe. Ein literarischer Führer
Eichborn Verlag, Berlin 2007

Ralf Roth
Das Jahrhundert der Eisenbahn
Jan Thorbecke Verlag, Ostfildern 2004

Beat H. Schweizer
Bahnen in Namibia
Trevor B Editions, Cape Town 2007

Brian Solomon
Railway Masterpieces
David &Charles, Newton Abbot 2002

Paul Theroux
The Great Railway Bazaar
Penguin, London, 1977

Wolstan Webb
Thirty years around the world
Adventures of a Railway Signals Engineer
Nyons, 1991

Web sites

General

Wikipedia (web sites on different stations)
www.de.wikipedia.org

Anecdotage.com (American site on anecdotes)
www.anecdotage.com

Darjeeling Himalaya Railway Society
http://www.dhrs.org/

Ferdinand Blumentritt
http://www.univie.ac.at/voelkerkunde/apsis/aufi/harry1.htm

The Indian Railways fan Club
http://www.irfca.org/

Statistics on railways of China
http://www.railwaysofchina.com/statistics.htm

Republic of Turkey, Ministry of Culture and Tourism
Ottoman capital Bursa- The railway
http://www.kultur.gov.tr/EN/BelgeGoster.aspx?17A16AE30572D31395FB1C518
0B6EBD69967B13382E62777

Skyscraper City
World´s Largest and Busiest Rail Stations
http://www.skyscrapercity.com/showthread.php?t=342415&page=41

Trains of Turkey
http://www.trainsofturkey.com/

The World Bank
Transport in South Asia
http://web.worldbank.org

Kim-Il Sung-Anecdote
http://north-korea.narod.ru/anecdotes.htm

Specific stations

Beijing railway
http://www.beijingimpression.com/beijing-guide/beijing-railway.shtml

Der Farang -In der Holzklasse nach Bangkok
http://www.der-farang.com/?article=2008/07/holzklasse

The China Post-Fenchihu
Fenchihu- a key scenic spot along Alishan railway
http://www.chinapost.com.tw/travel/taiwan-central/chiayi/2007/06/21/112984/Fenchihu-a.htm

Bombarding von Karagaac
http://www.military-quotes.com/forum/203992-post.html

Kishi Station and the Tama cat
http://www.japanprobe.com/2008/04/23/stationmaster-cat-draws-tourists/

Koolmannskuppe/Grasplatz
http://www.ingrids-welt.de/reise/nam/html/luederitzkolmanskopb.htm

Qingdao
http://english.sina.com/china/p/2008/0802/175525.html

Da Lat Station
http://www.funimag.com/photoblog/index.php/20090225/da-lat-train-station-solution-of-quiz-26/

Rangoon Station
http://www.myanmar.com/myanmartimes/MyanmarTimes18-343/n010.htm

Rockwood Cemetery, Sydney
http://en.wikipedia.org/wiki/Cemetery_Station_No._1_railway_station

Shengsing Station(Taiwan)
Welcome to Mialoi County Sanyi
http://www.sanyi.gov.tw/en/t01.htm

Meeting Inönü-Churchill in the station of Yenice
http://www.arkas.com.tr/english/pages/arkas_news/subat_2008/haber4.html

Picture sources

Bahnhof Beijing West (Cover-Rückseite)
http://en.wikipedia.org/wiki/File:Beijing_West_train_station_01.jpg
(Autor: Kim S., Creative Commons Attribute Share Alike 2.0 Generic license)

Bahnhof Bombay (Mumbai) CST
http://de.wikipedia.org/w/index.php?title=Datei:Shivaji_Terminus_Bomb ay_%28Mumbai%29.jpg&filetimestamp=20050702210736
(Photograph Sebastian Jude, GNU Free Documentation License ver. 1.2)

Bahnhof Chennai
http://en.wikipedia.org/wiki/File:ChennaiCentral2.JPG
(Urheber Swift Rakesh, Creative Commons Attribution-Share Alike 3.0 Unported license)

Bahnhof Dunedin
http://en.wikipedia.org/wiki/File:Dunedin_Railway_Station_Full_Exterio r.jpg
(Urheber: Antilived, Creative Commons Attribution-Share Alike 3.0 Unported license)

Bahnhof Istanbul Haydarpasa
http://en.wikipedia.org/wiki/File:Haydarpasa_train_station.jpg
(Urheber: Starliner, Lizenz GNU Free Documentation License ver. 1.2)

Bahnhof Howrah
http://en.wikipedia.org/wiki/File:Howrah.jpg
(Photograph Planara, GNU Free Documentation License ver. 1.2)

Bahnhof Melbourne
http://en.wikipedia.org/wiki/File:Flinders_street_train_station_melbourne .jpg
(Autor: Adam J.W.C, Creative Commons Attribution-Share Alike 2.5)

Bahnhof Pointe Noire
http://www.visoterra.com/photos-pointe-noire/la-gare-centrale.html

Bahnhof von Sylhet (Bangladesh, erste Innenseite)
http://sylhoti.multiply.com/photos/album/16/Beauty_of_sylhet#photo=28

Other railway station books of the author
(See www.bod.de, in total five volumes, 1001 stations)

Palace of a thousand winds and gooseberry station
Short stories about 222 railway stations in Germany
Books on Demand, Norderstedt 2020

The destiny station beyond the mountains
Short stories about 111 railway stations in the Alpine countries
Books on Demand, Norderstedt 2020

The cathedral of the winged wheel and the sugarbeet station
Short stories about 222 railway stations in Europe
Books on Demand, Norderstedt 2020

Grand Central Terminal and the station at the end of the world
Short stories about 222 railway stations of the Americas
Books on Demand, Norderstedt 2020

Istanbul-Haydarpasa station (Picture: Wikipedia)